BK-RAJAYOG, ROBIN SHARMA, MAGIC MANTRA FOR SUCCESS AND HEALTH

Dr. Dilip V. Kaundinya MD

[Ex-Professor and Head, Sir J J Hospital, Mumbai and Chairman of the MUHS committee for including Ethics and Spiritual Medicine in MBBS syllabus]

November 2018

BK-RAJAYOG, ROBIN SHARMA, MAGIC MANTRA FOR SUCCESS AND HEALTH

Dr. Dilip V. Kaundinya MD

[Ex-Professor and Head , Sir J J Hospital, Mumbai and Chairman of the MUHS committee for including Ethics and Spiritual Medicine in MBBS syllabus]

March 2019

First Published in 2019 by First Step Publishing

Editorial / Sales / Marketing Office at
303-304 Garnet Nirmal Lifestyles Ph 2
Behind Nirmal Lifestyles Mall
LBS Marg Mulund West
Mumbai 400080
E-Mail:- info@firststepcorp.com
www.firststepcorp.com

Copyright © Authors Copyright

All rights reserved. No part of this publication may be reproduced, stored in or introduced into a retrieval system of transmitted in any form or by any means (electronically, mechanically, photocopying, recording or otherwise) without the prior written permission of the author. Any person who does an unauthorized act in relation to this publication may be liable to criminal prosecution and civil claims for damages

ISBN:- 978-93-83306-49-7
Price: India INR 175
Rest $8
Donation to World Renewal Spiritual Trust of Brahma Kumaris, a NGO working for Global Peace, Health and Brotherhood

God's formula for Success
Be Ever Ready, Ever Alert, Ever Attentive, & Ever Active
with a high Passion Quotient for
Your Set Goal

1. Watch Peace of Mind Channel 24 x 7
2. Visit the nearest BK Center for a Free of Cost Foundation Course
3. 11500 BK Centers Across 140 Countries
4. Make BK Rajayoga a part of Daily Routine for health happiness and peace
5. Phone : - 09999333555 / 666 for nearest center

Table of Contents

Authors Heartfelt 8

INTRODUCTION 34

Chapter 1: Robin Sharma and the Wonderful Book – The Leader Who had No Title (LWT) 41

Chapter 2: Brahma Kumaris Rajayoga – A God Given Mantra for Health and Success 59

APPENDIX – I 92

APPENDIX – II 116

Authors Heartfelt

The main purpose of this book is to make the younger generation realize that ancient Patanjali sutra and Charak Sanhita are evidence based for health and performance enhancement. Dogmatism, divisionism, fanaticism and in the worst **case terrorism** are due to faulty interpretation of the tenets given in different religions. Spiritualism is a common thread that weaves through all the religions. Spiritualism and yogism are necessary for all human beings as the modern fast lifestyle has made the mankind to go against nature and lose the balance in all respects. **Internal balance is lost** giving loss of health, increased pollution and violence. **Global Consciousness Project** has proved that peace in the world could be restored by Mass Mind Intention using prayers and group meditation. **Tsunamis in mind result in the tsunamis of physical world.**

Quick burn out of the young and terrible addictions due to failures in life have become common. Balance between self- merit and expectations from life has been lost. Everybody wishes to own a Mercedes Benz. That is why spiritualism tells us that **all the desires are bad** as they give a restlessness syndrome till they are satisfied. Most funny part is that no sooner a desire is satisfied ,the second one immediately takes its place. **The culprit is the mind** which wants more and more. Patanjali Kriya yoga gives mind control [Mano-nigrah]. **Sleep-wake cycle** has been set against nature. Circadian bio-rhythms or Biological clock inside us has been set in accordance with sunrise and sunset since the origin of mankind. Our nocturnal habits have disturbed it so much that we require to learn "**Sleep hygiene**" merely to get a normal sound sleep. Sedatives become useless after some time. Ancient Vedas are actually scientific formula for leading our lives in accordance with unwritten but actually existing universal cosmic rules. **Laws of karma** are applicable to all human beings. Ignorance about them does not spare you from punishments. The horrific details of the punishment in proportion to Vikarma [Bad karma] are available in **Garud purana**. **Max Muller has said**- "There is no book in the world that is so thrilling, stirring and inspiring as the Upanishads.

German Physicist W. Heisenberg said-"After the conversations about Indian Philosophy, some of the ideas in Quantum Physics that had seemed crazy suddenly made much more sense." Current medical research highlights the value of asana, Pranayama, Dhyana and Dharana in health as well as man-management skills. **Ken Wilber's Transpersonal Psychology** talks about Atman to Atman transpersonal transactions for effective human resource management and development.

Spiritualism centres around metaphysical God and Atman or soul. Science has not been able to prove their existence. But that does not mean that these entities do not exist. Millions of people believe in their existence. **The definition of GOD** as Governing ,Operating, and Destroying and universally occupying benevolent healing energy becomes immediately acceptable to the **scientist minds**. But the Trinity of Brahma Vishnu and Mahesh immediately becomes labelled as **Indian mythology and myth**. God or Supreme Consciousness is the Supreme Creator, Operator and Destroyer Who creates the material world, provides energy to operate and maintain it and destroys whatever is evil or bad or effete and old. This super-duper scientist is running all the planets in all the galaxies in their pre-ordained orbits with **supreme accuracy** and without any exhaustible material fuel. No scientist till to this date has devised such a machinery. No wonder Sir Albert Einstein was made to say-"**Science is but an infant."** Microcosm of Dr Deepak Chopra is a part and parcel of vast Universal or Cosmic consciousness. Human Being is a **BMSO- Body Mind Soul Organism**. Body is Humus or soil. It comes from soil and goes to the soil. **Being is existence**. Being is indestructible, immortal, ageless and disease less soul. **Wellness** comes only when Being is happy. Body consciousness today is so prevalent that the whole focus of drugs and cosmetics is only on the body. **Core personality is forgotten**. Bhagavad Gita tells that all the sufferings in life[Bhog] arise out of body consciousness. Therefore it advises to attain a **soul conscious state of mind**. BK-Rajayoga for me became a practical manual for attaining soul consciousness and thereby get liberation from all the troubles and problems in life. This **exhaustive author's heartfelt** is an attempt to convince the younger generation to include BK-Rajayoga in their daily routine and experience for themselves that they had discovered a **Kalpa vruksha** that fulfils all of their desires -materialistic as well as spiritualistic. **Split second Decisions** give the most accurate solution to the problems or difficult situations. Health comes automatically. Success becomes a foregone conclusion.

Core personality or Atman or sukshma sharir is of prime importance. But we neglect it. One soul several bodies in different births is true. **Past Life Regression Hypnosis and Therapy[PLRH& T]** provides the scientific proof. Body is a costume suitable to our role as an actor in this world drama. **Sanchit karma**[Prarabhda or Karmic Account] decides our costume, our role and the quality of life we have in this birth. Thus the health, happiness, harmony, peace and success in life is **pre-ordained** and occurs as per Divine script which we write with our own hands. BK-Rajayoga gives hope and optimistic solution that your **Bad karmic Load could be burnt out in Yogagni** or fire of yoga and tapasya. Tasting is the proof of pudding. I have experienced it.

Greatest folly a man today commits is that he presumes and assumes the **role of a Doer** while in reality he is just an instrument in the hands of the divinity. In BK-Rajayoga Atman plays the music in tune with divine commandments called as **Shrimat obtained at each Bk-centre through Muralis, a four page script** read in all 11500 BK-centres in 140 countries. Atman in tune with Shrimat performs a spiritual effort[**purusharth**] to attain a Personality of Excellence[**Purushottam**] or more precisely a Brahma type of personality. Charak Sanhita describes 15 types of personalities[prakriti] depending on the level of consciousness. There are three main levels of consciousness- **Satvik, Rajasik** and **Tamasik**. **Brahma type** is the highest, purest, most knowledgeful and most powerful among the Satvik personalities. His soul is so powerful that it produces **a beneficial effect on the persons** in contact and purifies the whole atmosphere and nature with powerful and healing thought vibrations. Satanic or Asuri traits in the living beings get transformed into divine traits in a second. **Self-management and man-management** for such a person becomes very easy. He could mould others in accordance with his views. Success in any field becomes his birth right. **Vacha siddhi**, spoken words becoming a reality and **Sankalp siddhi**, the thoughts becoming an immediate reality becomes his usual and natural experience. The paintings of sages doing Tapasya and lions or tigers lolling harmlessly in front of them are not wild imagination but a scientific reality. Ever blissful state[**sat-chit-Anand state**] of consciousness manifests in his personality. Sthit-pragnya state of consciousness or a **state of spiritual equilibrium** becomes evident in such a personality. Grief and pleasure become equal to him in perception. There are eight levels of samadhi[**spiritual evolution**]. A level of 4 or above gives the power to materialize a golden Ganesh idol from thin air. Such super human powers are known as **Siddhis**. At seventh level beyond which eighth level **karmateet avastha** happens, a person comes to know the past, present and future in most precise and lucid terms. This is known as **Turia consciousness** or Trikaal darshee avastha. This is because the microcosm becomes perpetually connected to a cosmic google called cosmic consciousness. Brahma type personality has **two divine qualities [Divya Guna]**- Tejas or glow over the face and Ojas or a soul level attraction for other souls. BK-concepts describe this state as **Roohe gulab** which gives a charisma to the person.

Siddhis even give the power of par-kaya pravesh, kaya-kalpa [rejuvenation to young form], levitation, clairvoyance and astral travel. A book entitled "**Kriya babaji and 18 Yoga siddhas**" by a Canadian, Marshal Govindan and "**Autobiography of a yogi**" by Swamy Yoganand Paramhans describe different siddhas and their miraculous powers. **Maha Avatar Nagraj Babaji** is the first disciple of sixteenth yoga siddha ,Sage Patanjali. One thousand years old Kriya babaji is still existing in the body of a 16 years old young person for the guidance of yogis beyond a certain stage of attainment. Adi Shankaracharya was the first disciple of Kriya Babaji. He wrote a wonderful poem. The gist of the poem told- " Strange was the sight that a 16 years old person, sitting under a

Banyan tree and was teaching the aged disciples surrounding him. Still stranger was the fact that the whole transaction was taking place in total silence [without spoken words[**through thought vibrations**]. The discovery of Mirror neurons proves that silent transpersonal human transactions are possible through thought vibrations. The reason for this Atman to Atman attraction or **Ojas** is the presence of mirror neurons in each one of us. The thought vibrations emanating from the soul forms the body aura which could be visualized by Kirlian Body aura photography. BK Dr Chandrashekhar, who recorded a miraculous recovery from a widely spread cancer by **Volcanic Rajayoga Meditation,** made an ingenuous use of Universal Scanner for showing the blocks in Energy Chakras and for recording the span of body aura. **Ojas is a divine quality** [Divya guna] that arises out of the presence of exceptional Right and Left Brain coherence as shown by EEG[Electro Encephalogram]. Such person also has unique and extra ordinary **empathy [samavedana]** for other persons. This Emotional Intelligence or a high EQ[Emotional Quotient] gives an uncanny ability to know by intuition where the other man's shoe is pinching. At the same time such person does try to remove this grief to the best of his ability and give immediate solace to the other person. Such quality creates a natural bonding between the two individuals. The persons then may risk even their lives to save such a philanthropic person. This is the most important quality in **a Leader without title.** The people become his automatic and willing followers. Today in the higher posts of administration, Emotional Intelligence[EQ] is more valued than high Intelligence Quotient. Women have a natural and greater Right -Left brain coherence . No wonder they are the leaders who occupy high positions in almost every organization. Regular practice of BK-Rajayoga confers this increased coherence in men also. Emotional Intelligence is very important in man-management, Human Resource Development[HRD] and in **healthy doctor-patient relationship**. Development of just one divine quality shall reduce the incidence of court cases and assaults on the doctors. But Western medicine lacks a consciousness based approach and so doctors today have become money making machines in a majority of the cases. Greed has been ingrained in doctors as well as Pharma companies.

Magical advances in science and in the field of Artificial Intelligence **[AI]** has conferred miraculous improvement in Working

Intelligence**[WI] of the robots**. But the best of scientists in the field of AI have not been able to inculcate Emotional Intelligence in the robots. These brilliant scientists frankly admit that their lack of understanding of the **phenomenon called as Consciousness** is responsible for this vital deficiency. Roger Sperry who got Nobel prize in 1970 for his concept of "One brain and two minds" tells that the Scientist mind in the dominant hemisphere is the root cause of the lack of Emotional Intelligence and most of the problems we face in this world. **This culprit mind** is judgemental about other persons and often finds faults in others. It self-centric and ego-driven. It wants to command and does not know how to mould. It is calculating and its relationships with other persons are based **on self-gains. It** likes to hear its own voice and often has a deaf ear for sound advice. It runs after higher and higher achievements often at the cost of others and its own health. **Winning in Rat race** and cut throat competition against faith and religious and spiritual tenets bring positive outcomes for a short while. But soon they get replaced with stark failures. Their **self-centric** nature[vrutti] creates a negative impact on the workers underneath such persons. **Scientist Mind** is the seat of negativity. It is always full of negative thoughts like lust, anger,

Ego, Greed, jealousy, hatred, doubt and repulsion. Today it is filled with stress, anxiety, tension, apprehension, fear worry and frustration out of its failure due to **comparison and competition** with others. Positive thoughts and healing emotions hardly ever arise in such a soul. It requires scientific proof before it can believe and have faith even in the God. Such persons firmly believe that they are self-made men forgetting that with such statements they relieve the Almighty of a terrible responsibility. **Spiritualist Mind** in the other hemisphere functions on belief, faith and positive thoughts and emotions. Philanthropy comes automatically to such persons. Spiritualist mind is the **sleeping giant** lying dormant in all of us. It has immense potential in terms of wisdom, experience and power. The experiences of past several births are stored in this mind. BK Rajayoga silences the internal noise in the Dominant hemisphere or Scientist Mind .This phase has been termed as Internal silence **[Antar mauna]** by the sages. The first and foremost quality this internal silence confers is an extraordinary ability of **Samyak shravana** [Holistic hearing] in which whole of the consciousness is focused on the act of listening. People could remember Veda by merely listening to them once [Ekpathy] because of this extra ordinary ability. The spiritualist Mind is a **super**

computer. It tallies the present problem with the data of "Experiences" from the past several births and springs out a **solution almost instantaneously**. This is intuition or gut feeling or inner voice. The uncanny wisdom of going for an **"Extra mile"** comes from this mind. Out of world paintings and innovations come from this mind. Self-determination, self-discipline and self-dedication for achieving a noble goal comes from this mind. This mind also gives a very meaningful **S.W.O.T. analysis**. It makes us realize our hidden potentials and strengths and also the weaknesses. Specific autosuggestions and visualization programme in Bk-Rajayoga removes the weaknesses and potentiate our strengths. Most important is that it confers an ability to differentiate between Opportunity and threat. Many times the threats in life come disguised as wonderful opportunity and the opportunity comes in the form of a threat. A wrong decision at this point of time means great loss or immense gain. Silence of Scientist Mind confers the ability to have an **accurate decision** in such matters. In spite of dominance of Scientist Mind first two seconds of silent transaction between the Mirror Neurons gives the most accurate judgement about the person or an event. This is the weak voice of Spiritualist Mind to help us. But in the **ever present ego** of a person makes him say " Let me think over it." Normally all the thinking is done by the dominant scientist mind. So even after a deliberate delay occurring because of thinking and having **second thoughts**, we take a wrong decision. This is known as **"Harding Error"** that may come in way of snap two second judgements by the Spiritualist Mind.. That is why intuition means listening to your inner voice with more care and attention. Harding error arises out of bodily charms of the other person. Person falls in love at first and then goes on repenting for whole of the life. Harding error is the root cause of divorces within six months of marriage in the younger generation today. Body consciousness brings the error in judgement though an Inner voice has protested.

Self-experience is the best teacher in the world. So here I shall elaborate the importance of BK-Rajayoga practice for health and self enhancement based on **my experiences** in life. I hope and trust that they shall form a **guiding beacon** for younger generation in the present turbulent times. A sharp Saraswat Mind, meritorious educational achievements and self confidence saw me becoming Professor and Head at a very early age of 31 years in Government institution. This was nothing less than a miracle for a Brahmin in reservation oriented system. So my natural conclusion was that I shall retire as the Director of Medical Education and Research. But **God had others plans for me**. So a very apt prayer should always tell God-" Please do not give me **what I desire**. But give me what You plan to give me in life because You know best what is best for me." Bhagavad Gita tells the same thing in different way-" Before time and above the fate no one gets in anything in life."

My posting at Swami Ramanand Teerth Rural Medical College at Taluka place called Ambejogai in the most backward Beed District was the turning point. A **phase of intense problems** began. I was promoted to the post of Professor and Head in 1981. But malignant cast politics of unimaginable intensity made me a victim. An acting and most corrupt Dean of a particular powerful category facing numerous enquiries due to gross financial irregularities, wrote adverse CRs out of jealousy and fear that I may rob his post. He went on taking out his venom for nine years. **This was against rules. Adverse CRs have to be communicated in the same year so that one gets adequate notice** to show improvement. The result in 1992 was that I was demoted to the post of Associate Professor on which I was promoted by MPSC selection **in 1973**.

Once again Divinity intervened. A Matt judgement and efforts of **Late Gopinath Mundeji and Pramodji** reversed the reverses immediately so that I remained a Professor with a proverbial Damocles' sword of demotion and transfer hanging over my head. The complete justice was done in **1996 killing all of my chances even to become a Dean.** Thus I missed becoming the Director. BK-concepts and also Bhagavad Gita tell us that "Every moment of the word drama is most accurate and most beneficial. Whatever has happened is good. Whatever that is happening is better and whatever shall that happen in future shall be the best." At that point of time it was difficult for me to swallow this **spiritual wisdom.** My mind kept on asking – **"Why me"?** Retrospectively when I introspect , I realized that every word of wisdom was accurately correct. Had I been promoted as the Director, I would have spent all the remainder of my service kissing the feet of greedy politicians. The **quantum jump in the Quality of Life** I am experiencing after adopting BK-Rajayoga in my daily routine, would never would have come my way. I must narrate some more incidences to prove my point. A transfer from **rural medical college** to advanced tertiary care hospital in **Mumbai** would have devasted many lesser souls. Brain of a Saraswat gave me the fame as examiner who asks tricky and very meaningful questions. At the same time generosity which probably I developed in **the Sangam Yug[Era of confluence]** of previous birth kept me generous with marks. In fact I used to assure each and everybody that your passing marks you have already earned by your mere presence. Answers to questions shall differentiate a distinction holder. **Dr Mrs Kaundinya ,Professor and Head of Physiology, was most popular amongst students as her teaching made** the subject very easy. Students' feedback always told that Microbiology and Physiology are the best departments in teaching. At one of point of time there were as many as **14 distinctions is Microbiology**. In our times Distinctions were rare and exceptionally brilliant person used to get it. So a question arose- Are the students so brilliant or our teaching is out of this world? My mind told me that these two could be contributing factors. **But real performer** is MUHS pattern of examinations with **MCQ, BAQ, SAQ and set of FAQs[** Multiple choice questions, Brief Answer Questions, Short answer questions and Frequently asked questions.] In short it was made very difficult for the student to fail. At the same time setting of the question paper became an **ordeal for the examiners**. Many appointed their juniors privately for such onerous tasks and of course with nothing more than good will which helped in postgraduate examinations. **Dr Dongaokar the first VC** took lifelong and more than adequate revenge over the examiners and medical teachers. The vacations also became reduced to half. **A hell has been created for the medical teachers** and the examiners. Slightest mistake in filling the complicated mark sheets became an offense under **UNFAIR MEANS** and the poor examiner has to report to Nasik at his own expenses like a **hardened criminal reporting to police station where the clerks donned role of a judge.** At MUHS after a wait of several hours revelation used to come that a countersignature was required on a particular page. **Not a single Vice chancellor has made an effort to change the harassing rules for the examiners and a paltry sum as remuneration.** BK Rajayoga gave such mind empowerment that I did not have to face any such ordeals because of the focus.

Immense stress gave me seven incurable diseases ranging from chronic cough, cervical spondylitis, Thyrotoxicosis, Chronic fatigue, severe back pain due to Spondylolisthesis, tendoachilles tear while practising for veteran tournament and almost a burn out. **Bk-Rajayoga gave impossible and permanent cures.**

Saraswats are God fearing and highly superstitious. BK-Rajayoga gave **emancipation** from several false beliefs and superstition. One of these I must mention. I used to worry on two counts while on the Path of Bhakti.

1] I used to fear that my non-vegetarian food habits surely shall give me a birth in the Yoni of a tiger. Once that happens how I shall hope to become grass eating tiger? Otherwise how I could come back to **human yoni?**

2] Secondly everybody these days is telling that **kayamat or Pralaya** or final deluge is very nearby. How painful it shall be to die by drowning?
Muralis which are from mystical experiences to a human conduit Brahma Baba removed these major fears. God Himself assured that a human being always takes the birth of a human being. Secondly, India i.e. Bharat never goes under the water as Incorporeal God Shiva always takes Avataran only in Bharat.

Another most assuring part was that God assured repeatedly in His Muralis that He will move with a protective umbrella over your head provided you always remain busy in His remembrance. The **Yogagni** [Fire of Meditation] shall burn out all of your Bad karmic Load and emancipate you from pain and suffering. I have several personal experiences about these novel guarantees by the Supreme Father of all the souls.

The "Experiences" and divine Muralis helped to set an **elevated goal for myself**. Geriatric OPD in Sir J J Hospital revealed to me the End stage battle of the soul before final emancipation as a consequence of unfinished Karmic Load. The visits to old age homes revealed **the hell** that awaits us if we do not shed our bad Karmic load by intense spiritual effort[**Purusharth**].

Interactions with **AYUSH and NCD wing** of Director of Health Services since **2012** revealed the horrible plight of doctors and of everybody in this horrible era called as Iron age[Kali yug] due to stress born NCDs[Non-infectious Chronic Diseases]. **NCDs are non-stop CDs of pain and sufferings**. They include diseases ranging from Obesity, acidity, insomnia , Diabetes, Depression and Heart attacks to cancers, Parkinsonism and Dementia. Suicides, Burn out and addictions are the common consequences. Sometimes the pain and suffering is so intense that there is a cry for **euthanasia or mercy killing.**

Another very serious problem is that noble healthcare profession has become **five star sickness care Industry.** Firstly fall ill and then we shall take care of you at an astronomical cost of course to compensate for our troubles. Falling ill has become a crime for a common man because his illness may devastate the family financially and permanently. No wonder an exodus has begun towards Complimentary Alternative Medicine[**CAM**] which are beyond any control like that by FDA. So several unfortunate people are becoming **victims of quackery**. Modern Medicine promptly declares all such modalities of treatment as " **Pseudoscience" without** making any effort to test the claims of cure by CAMs.

My "experiences" with BK-Rajayoga gave me firm belief that "**An awakening** " of both the doctors and the common man is necessary to make Bk-Rajayoga as evidence based panacea for all illnesses. BK- Rajayoga is an easy meditation for very busy people today.So Divine Plan made me the chairman of a novel MUHS committee to include "**Ethics and Spiritual Medicine in MBBS syllabus" in the year 2013.**

First problem was the absence of a book that gives consciousness based approach to health and cure- which modern medicine calls as **The Whole Person**

Medicine. Supreme Teacher got a book entitled **"Spiritual Medicine for modern lifestyle diseases,"** written by me in the year 2013 itself in mere 21 days while at Bengaluru. This book then went through obstacle race from 2013 to 2018 for getting published. Funny part was that the whole of medical wing of Brahma kumaris felt that my book is not worth publishing by the BK-Literature department. But a **miraculous Divine plan** reached the book to all the International BK-Centres due to **BK Amola Shah of Florida**. Second edition is now getting published by **First Step Publishers in 2019**. A review of the book appeared in Antiseptic Journal in **December 2018.** In the same month, review article entitled – "Meditation versus Relaxation" by myself and Dr Mrs. S. D. Kaundinya got published in the International Journal of Basic and APPLIED Physiology. All of these are miracles in accordance with a Divine script.

Now the next target was to prepare a **short add-on syllabus in spiritual medicine so that MCI permission should not become necessary.** Syllabus submitted in May 2013 became modified to mere **five lectures and five "Experiential sessions"** to be conducted only in the first Academic term of three subjects- **Physiology** at First MBBS level, **Forensic Medicine** at Second MBBS level and **General**

Medicine at Final MBBS level. Every care was taken so that the syllabus should not be a burden to the students. Secondly the medical students shall have a prolonged and perpetual exposure for the entire tenure in a medical college of four and half years, to three evidence based mindfulness meditation-

1] Vipassana of Buddhism 2] Preksha Dhyana of Jainism and 3] BK-Rajayoga. The students shall be able to decide which meditation suits them best for their stress management and performance enhancement. Present VC Dr Dileep Mhaisekar had put up the syllabus for discussion in Academic Council in **June 2017. But medically illiterate majority did not allow the VC to implement the recommendations at MUHS level and forced him to submit it to MCI for permission. Today MCI stands dissolved.**

A fresh struggle to implement the syllabus in spiritual Medicine began **in 2019.** The following eminent personalities in the field of medicine have given the foreword for my book-
1] Padma Bhushan **Dr R. D. Lele,** Director of the division of Nuclear medicine, 2]Padmashree **Dr Alaka Deshpande** Professor and Head of Medicine and central Nodal officer for AIDS control 3] **Dr Yusuf Matcheswala** Honorary Professor of Psychiatry at Sir J J Hospital , Mumbai 4] **Dr Naras**

Bhat, Professor of Mind Body Medicine, Seybrook University, Sanfrancisco, USA and 5] **Dr Sujal Shah** a renowned Retinal specialist and the President of Jain Doctors" Federation. All of them sent letters to Honourable Academic Council of MUHS recommending the acute need of including Spiritual Medicine in MBBS syllabus. They have pointed out that **USA** has started undergraduate and post graduate courses in Spiritual Medicine in the year 2001 itself soon after **WHO** added spiritual health in its definition of total Health in the year 1998. Other developed countries have followed USA. But India ie Bharat

Is minimum of 18 years behind the world. A great Nation which made the whole world celebrate **International Yoga day on every 21st June** is so much behind in implementing a thoughtful recommendation for bringing a better tomorrow in the present Health scenario, is both **shameful and retrogressive.**

Another very pertinent fact is that the demand for teaching and training in spiritual medicine has been ascertained from the medical students and the specialists by **two CMEs on " Value of spiritual and yogic strategies in modern medicine"** in Sir J J Hospital, Mumbai held in January 2014 and March 2014. Both the KAP study [Knowledge Aptitude and Practice] and Feedback study on two CMEs have been published in medical journal.

A majority [98 per cent] of participants opined as under-
1] They know that spiritual and yogic practices are necessary for their health and stress management. But they are in absolute confusion. There are multiple yoga systems and each one tells it is the best amongst all. Many come in commercial packages. So the mind is unable to decide.
2] They shall never depend upon non-medical self-**proclaimed spiritual Gurus** to learn Yogic practices. They shall always prefer teaching and training by a trained member of teaching Faculty. **Such Faculty which has official recognition could only be created once the spiritual medicine gets incorporated in MBBS syllabus.**

If Dr Mhaisekar succeeds in his ceaseless efforts then MUHS shall be the first Medical University in India which has followed USA and other advanced countries in bringing the syllabus to **global standards**. **NCD wing** shall have adequately trained doctors to apply meditation as therapeutic strategy. Alarming rise of NCDs in young population shall be checked and may be eradicated. Health Budget of Maharashtra could be drastically reduced. My dream of "My India, Healthy, Happy and addiction free India" shall become a reality.

Robin Sharma has given excellent recipe for success in life in his two very wonderful books.. But they become practical and applicable only if person has an empowered mind **and** health by regular practice of BK-Rajayoga. The book "The monk who sold his Ferrari" describes an American advocate who was busy enjoying everything fast in his life. One day he collapses in the court room with massive heart attack. His doctor gave him two alternatives- "Leave the practice to live well or continue with the practice and drop dead eventually." The advocate wanted to go to Himalayas .So he sold his practice to his assistant. The first chapter begins with the assistant burning the midnight oil when a 30 years old person forcefully enters his chamber. The assistant mistook this person to be the son of his former employer. As it turned out the former employer himself was standing before him. I am sure this kaya kalpa[Magical rejuvenation] has happened because of the kriya yoga that sages in Himalaya taught him. Robin Sharma has not elaborated on this aspect. The second book gives magical formulae for success in life by discovering a leader sleeping silently in all of us. But I believe that these formulae shall never succeed in bringing out the desired transformation unless and until help of daily BK-Rajayoga is taken. The much needed self-determination, self-dedication and self-discipline comes only sadhana of BK Rajayoga.

12 March 2019
Dr D.V. Kaundinya MD

INTRODUCTION

The time cycle has not four but five phases. The last one called Age of confluence [Sangam yug] was revealed to me after seven days' foundation course in Rajayoga at a Meditation Hut in Sir J J Hospital campus. Why incorporeal God, Shiv chose sir J J Hospital in Mumbai to have a Rajayoga hut? Answer to me was obvious. An exceptionally philanthropic soul donated his life time's saving for creation of this divine campus. An independent Parsee Geriatric ward takes care of end stage sufferings of an erring human being. This ward actually makes us visualize our future prior to death. Bad Karmic load is very real and not a myth. Each soul regardless of his or her religion has to shed this accumulated huge load in this last birth for all of us in two ways-1] by undergoing sufferings sometime so intense that the soul cries out for euthanasia in ignorance. Even if you cut short your sufferings by euthanasia the unfinished karmic load is carried out to the next birth. An infant who hardly had a chance to perform any karma suffers due to congenital anomalies is the proof for unfinished karmic account. You may ask in wonder is there a next birth? Past Life Regression Hypnosis and Therapy [PLRH & T] provides the scientific truth. One soul and several different bodies in different births is not a myth. In fact true history of India begins from 5000 years ago. Ramayana and Mahabharata are not mythology but the glorious history of India which is never taught in school syllabus. We never study our own great and real heroes. We read and know only what Moguls and British allowed us to read and know. Visit the various historical places in north, south, west and east of India and the guide reveals to us our glorious past. Bharat was not what a caricature depicts in the modern maps. King Ranjitsinh has conquered Afghanistan. Burma, Australia and Africa were inseparable part of India. Geological drift moved these countries away from India. Lord Krishna, Lord Rama all of them are as real as Lord Gautama Buddha. All of them were highly evolved, enlightened and very powerful souls. Patanjali sutra 2500 years ago described yog-siddha souls who could undertake astral travel. Shiva lingams have been found in the deepest forest of Amazon recently where no human being has gone till to this date. This is an obvious proof for the ability of yog-siddhas for astral travel.

Greek, Egyptian, Zoroastrian and Indian mythology, all describe a golden age in which a golden race [having kanchan kaya] ruled the earth. Several recent studies in Journal of Consciousness have proved that more than 18500 human genes have mutated in last two decades to give an emergence of a race very much superior in intelligence forcing the psychiatrists to modify the older IQ scales. The geniuses with the previous scale come in the lowest five rungs in the present scale. But superior intellect is a double edged weapon in the present era called Iron Age in which the devil, Maya, Ravana or Shaitan is most powerful and launches his last and most virulent attack for survival. The soul in this era is at its weakest. So it easily succumbs to "honey trap" and "Money trap". The weakness of the soul could be inferred from a novel "Happiness Index Machine" devised by BK Dr. Chandrasekhar. A powerful soul full of purity and soul consciousness is always happy [Sat-Chitta-anand or ever blissful state of consciousness]. Weak soul easily leaves the Straight Path, Path of Shreyas or Sirat al mustaqim and starts traversing on the Path of Devil full of material gains and attractions. Thus begins a slow but sure journey to a phase of intense pain and sufferings [Bhog]. Ego of science makes the doctors to disbelieve in ancient Indian art and science of healing. Thomas Babington Macaulay has done a permanent damage to Indian psyche [Vrutti] which even today after so many decades of independence firmly believes that whatever is British or foreign is good and greater than our own. As the chairman of the MUHS committee I got a chance to address high level doctors at world famous Haffkine Institute, Sir J J Hospital in Mumbai and several medical colleges and research Institutions in Maharashtra. Uniformly doctors refused to believe that **Vrutti nirodh**, or transformation of the psyche is possible by Patanjali Kriya yog or Indian Integral Yog practices with the understanding of wisdom and knowledge in five thousand years old Bhagavad Gita. Kriya yog appears as huge chapter in Textbooks of Physiology describing this ancient art and science of healing for maintenance of health and conquest over ageing. Bhagavad Gita today is considered as the most powerful book on psychotherapy which revived grossly depressed Arjuna in the quickest possible time. BK-Rajayoga is the easy and most practical remix of knowledge from Bhagavad Gita and Patanjali sutra. It describes an easy meditation for busy people of modern times. It is evidence based for health, self-empowerment and self-enhancement. The single pointed focus of consciousness [Ekagra chitta avastha] performs miracles in the field of health, quick learning [education], man-management, time management and self-management leadership [SML]. BK-Rajayoga knowledge has been received through mystical experiences to an evolved and enlightened person who was chosen as conduit for transmitting the true knowledge by the Incorporeal God. Doctors raise a grave doubt about the knowledge as Mystical experiences and hallucinations occur in the same area of the cerebral cortex. Unshakable belief and faith are the quickest methods to proceed on a journey of thousand miles. Roger Sperry in 1970 described the concept of one brain and two minds. Spiritualist mind is the subconscious mind which functions on belief and faith. But the Scientist Mind in dominant hemisphere is rational, logical and demands hard scientific evidence to have belief and faith. Psychiatrists today, describe "Scientism", a malady which probable shall demand a DNA certificate from the parents to believe that they are really its parents. Dr. N. N. Wig, the world renowned Professor emeritus of Psychiatry and the only Indian to receive the fellowship of prestigious Royal Society Psychiatrists, London, described

"Spiritual vacuum" as the root cause of all the physical and mental illnesses today. Current researches in institutes of Mind Body Medicine in USA support the spiritual concepts in Veda. Vedanta denotes a phase when the soul, Ekpathy, Dwipathy or Tripathy, has a diminution of memory. It no more could remember the Vedas taught by word of mouth. Written script appeared. Vedas indicate the beginning of Copper age [Dwaper]. Golden and silver eras were of deities who were fully soul-conscious and had highest state of purity. Pushpak viman an aero machine flying on the strength of powerful laser beam thoughts is not a myth as proved by research in several Russian Institutes. One must read "Source Field investigations, by David Wilcock" to know the miraculous research conducted by R& D institutes in Russia. Faraday cage experiment shows that the thought vibrations could travel an infinite distance and could give desired effects. Thus third grade Reiki is not a myth. BK-Rajayoga technique is an evidence based method for self-transformation by thought-transformation. An evolved soul could bring world transformation by his thought power [Sankalpa Shakti]. All of this may be as difficult to prove by scientific methods as to show sweetness in sugar. Whole of spiritual knowledge is based on conglomerate of "Experiences" and "Mystical Experiences" of evolved souls. Science was never involved. So today we have

two types of evidences-1] Experiential evidence and 2] Experimental evidence". Experiential evidence" brings God in front of you in a second. But the scientific evidence to prove the existence of just one God's particle, Higgins's boson required years of research and huge expenses. Total trusting surrender and faith is the only criterion required for having an instantaneous belief in the existence of God.

Self-realization is the most effective method for various types of managements-Time, resources, management and stress management as it increases focus, S.W.O.T. analysis and out of box thinking. BK-Rajayoga gives us the Self-Management Leadership skills [SML].

Chapter 1: Robin Sharma and the Wonderful Book – The Leader Who had No Title (LWT)

The book entitled "The monk who sold his Ferrari" by Robin Sharma impressed me greatly. It describes a miraculous rejuvenation of a famous advocate who dropped down in a courtroom due to a massive heart attack. Doctor gave two choices- Leave the practice or drop dead eventually. Advocate chose rightly and went to Himalayas which was his fondest dream. Though the author had not elaborated on ancient Patanjali Kriya yog, I am sure the advocate went training in this this Indian Integral Yog in Himalayas where the true sages exist even today. Kriya yog or Ashtang yog consists of Yama, Niyama, Asana, Pranayama, Dhyan, Dharana, Pratyahar and Samadhi. Sage Patanjali clearly tells Samadhi does not mean dissolution into God but emancipation from pain and suffering in life by conquest of ageing, grey hair, dim vision and diseases. Souraba Samadhi denotes conquest of death. I personally do not belief in conquest of death. But 1000 years old Maha Avatar Nagraj Babaji or Kriya Babaji is believed to be still alive in the body of a 16 year old with a definite divine purpose. It is a belief that Babaji appears for further guidance when one has reached a certain stage of spiritual enlightenment and evolution. Spiritual ladder is supposed to be consisting of eight levels. A person acquires Siddhis or super natural powers at third or fourth stage. In fact siddhis are supposed to be an attack by micro form of Maya or Devil. It makes you lose the sight of final goal of spiritual effort [Purusharth]. BK-Rajayoga specifies that the final goal of spiritual effort is to achieve deity like status in Purity or to develop a personality of purity. One thousand years old Charak sanhita describes 15 types of personalities. Highest, purest and most powerful personality is called as Brahma type. Dada Lekhraj, an internationally famous diamond merchant in Karachi became famous as Brahma Baba after mystical experiences revealed the true and ultimate knowledge to him. Holy Quran came into existence in the same fashion. That is why only two religions in the whole world are described as True Art of Living or Way of Life-Hinduism and Islam.

Let us now revise some of the most powerful lines Robin uses in his wonderful book for achieving success. He mentions that remaining fit is very important for becoming and remaining as a leader. He prescribes getting up at 5am so that you get an extra one or two hours as bonus .The whole world sleeps while you plan your day with vividness and precision. BK-Rajayoga prescribes getting up at 4am, the amrit vela. Brahma muhurta or amrit vela begins from 2.30 am and ends at 4.45 am. I am getting up at 3.30 am as per the practice at Mount Abu, a truly divine place for pilgrimage. The atmosphere in this time slot called Amrit vela. In this period is rejuvenating and it is more so at Madhuban or Mount Abu. Some as yet not accepted research has proved that one gets the maximum benefit out of cosmic healing vibrational whisper during this magical period of time. The all pervasive benevolent cosmic energy in the form of this whisper brings about miraculous rejuvenation while passing through seven energy chakras in the body.. Alchemy of God, a group of brilliant BK scientists proved the existence, size and aura of God and soul by applying the Pythagorean principles in sacred geometry. They conclude that the aura of God is vast and pervasive throughout the all the galaxies of Universe.

The mantras for success in life given in the book entitled "The leader who had not title" by Robin Sharma are excellent to read. But when the time comes for bringing them into practice, a most essential quality one has to have is the self-discipline. BK-Rajayoga is a self-management leadership [SML] which enhances the will power and gives an ability to transform words into action. The mantras are as under

1] It is easy to sleep. But getting up early in the morning gives you a clear start of minimum of two hours before the whole world wakes up. There shall be plenty of time to sleep once you are dead. BK-Rajayoga advises to get up at 4am which is known as Amrut vela or Brahma muhurta. In Islam Tahjud Ki namaz begins at 4am and is said to be most powerful. In this specific time slot which begins at 2.30 am and ends at 4.45 am there is no impendence in establishing the connection with the Supreme Consciousness and it is easy to achieve a "Single pointed focus of thoughts" in seconds.

2] Repetition is a powerful technique. A new idea could quickly become integrated as new belief. Two powerful techniques of mind empowerment are used in BK-Rajayoga-1] autosuggestion and 2]

visualization. These two techniques are the basis of psychotherapy and cognitive behavioural change. Neuroscience studies have proved that if any one positive thought [sankalpa] is repeated several times in a day for mere 21 days then it transforms the nature [Vrutti] according to the autosuggestion given. Regular practice of BK-Rajayoga makes you discover the centre of strength that lies within you. Rajayoga practice quietens the turbulent scientist min in the judgemental dominant hemisphere of the brain. This is the internal silence [Antar mauna] about which ancient Indian sages talk about in the scriptures. Then the Spiritualist Mind in the other hemisphere takes charge of the functioning. This mind works on unshakable belief and faith. Two seconds decisions or snap judgements by this mind are most accurate. Life become very easy and all the work is carried out automatically and smoothly. For example-Initially when you learn car driving the continuous instructions from the dominant mind confuse you. Then you press accelerator instead of the break. Once the memory is embedded firmly in the silent hemisphere car driving becomes easy and automatic. The Spiritual Mind is the store house of wisdom and experience gathered through past innumerable births.

3] Set the goal after deep contemplation and study. Then bring some forceful emotion, energy and passion into the equation for realizing your goal. Programme your mind with a single powerful thought for achieving your gaol. This technique called as Neurolinguistic Programming [NLP] by a psychiatrist Dr. Watson generates a Passion Quotient. BK-Rajayoga meditation involves setting a goal, neuro-linguistic programming to generate Passion Quotient for attaining a novel and out of box goal-to achieve a deity like status of consciousness.

4] Robin Sharma tells to identify this inner leader within you. BK-Rajayoga gives the true identity of this Inner Leader, the Atman or soul a metaphysical entity that could be seen only when the Third Eye [Divya chakshu] gets opened. Neuroscience today believes that the seat of soul is tiny pineal gland situated in the axis drawn from the centre of the eyebrows. Pineal gland today is known as Spiritual eye. Another astonishing feature is that this gland has the internal structure like that of human eye. A gland surrounded on all sides by brain tissue and in complete darkness has a machinery to process Photons or Light Energy Particles. Why? Greek, Egyptian and Indian philosophies believe that Pineal gland is God's antenna used by the Messengers of God to receive celestial messages. The Divine Messages possibly in the form of vibrations are converted into light energy particles and then perceived by the pineal gland. In short Vedas and scriptures are full of such unbelievable information which the infant science may take any number of years to prove scientifically. Belief and faith in metaphysical entities generates a transcendental or extra-terrestrial state of consciousness and may be responsible for mystical experiences [sakashtkars]. But the problem is that in BMSO or Body Mind Soul Organism or a human being is a super duper car manufactured by a Supreme Intelligence. So the hallucinations [Bhrum] and the mystical experiences occur in the same area of cerebral cortex. Most common question from doctors is that how to differentiate between two different manifestations of the same consciousness? My answer to them is God Only Knows.[GOK]. Now several newer diseases have emerged where in spite of the state of art advanced technologies fail to reveal any abnormality. All of these ailments now are commonly known as GOK diseases. God is sending googlies to the ego driven doctors.

5] Robin Sharma tells that success does not happen because of stars. It is something that is consciously created by a conscious choice not to play victim of circumstances. It is impossible to build a monument of success on the foundation of excuses. Victims recite problems. Leaders present solution. But the greatest problem here is that one requires unshakable faith in your vision and unrelenting confidence in one's own ability to bring about a positive transformation. BK-Rajayoga gives power of transformation by regular practice. Soul is a powerful transmitter of thought vibrations. The persons with negative nature [Vrutti] in extreme cases become psychic energy vampires drawing strength from the stronger colleagues. But an empowered soul could bring about the transformation of other persons in the vicinity and also of the nature [Prakruti] and atmosphere. The tsunamis of nature occur because of the violent turbulent mass human consciousness in the present times. BK Rajayoga turns the mind into a serene lake without any turmoil. This power of silence has to be experienced for believing in it. We often saw in the pictures that show the sages are doing meditation [Tapasya] and the lions and tigers are lolling about in front of them. Today I believe that this could be possible as the serene but powerful thought vibrations must be having a calming effect on violent animal species. Divine Body aura around the sages used to protect their residential premises from devilish or satanic entities. Kirlian Body aura photography of Dadi Janaki , the International Head of Brahma kumaris , revealed that it goes beyond the recording plate with deepening stages of meditation. Her EEG[electro encephalogram] always shows deep and slowest delta waves of deep sleep in awakened state. So she has been certified as the most stable mind in the whole world. Bhagavad Gita describes this state of consciousness as the state of spiritual equilibrium [Sthit¬pragnya avastha].

6] Stop making excuses. Take responsibility to bring about a change in mind set [Vrutti] and push for excellence. The first essential step is self-transformation. The world transformation happens automatically and easily by looking at you as an example. Assume total responsibility for your actions and their consequences. Remember nobody succeeds beyond his or her wildest expectations unless he or she begins with some wild expectations. Bk-Rajayoga practice gives this courage of conviction.

7] Einstein had said-"Great spirits have always encountered severe opposition from mediocre minds." So forget about what others might say. Good and innovative people construct monuments with the stones their critics throw at them. It is when nobody criticises you that you should get worried. BK-Rajayoga teaches you to sidetrack any obstruction or opposition or to fly over it.

8] Expect more from yourself than anyone around you could ever expect from you. This is known as going for an extra mile. It requires courage of conviction and belief in your own thinking. Remember there is lot less of competition at extra mile. BK-Rajayoga enhances self -belief and self-esteem.

9] Always have passion for creativity and renovation. Never try to repackage a formula. All people want fresh value and noel forms of excellence. They certainly do not want repackaging. Innovate to work better and faster to yield more output.

10] Your "Thought choices" decide your performance. Remove all the waste and negative thoughts which raise obstructions of your own creation on way to achieving your goal. Your "Positive mental architecture" is important. BK-Rajayoga re-writes the corrupted and negatively transcribed CD of your mind by infusing fresh and positive thoughts which get embedded in your subconscious mind or psyche. These implanted seeds sprout under appropriate adverse circumstances or sudden obstruction that may arise on way of realization and achieving your goal in life. Focussed effort and consistent practice of minimum ten years is the formula for world class success.

11] Dream big yet start small. Daily ripples of superior thoughts and daily small improvements over time lead to stunning results as a cumulative effect. BK-Rajayoga practice is the example for this pearl of wisdom from Robin Sharma.

12] Never postpone or procrastinate as the procrastination is a form of fear. The FEAR means False Evidence taken as real. Supreme Soul in His divine Muralis always tells the same thing. No sooner you get a Sankalpa [Positive thought] act upon it immediately. It is my experience that a good thought vanishes entirely from the mind if a delay of even twenty hours delay has happened in taking the action.

13] Focus on your health. Excellent ideas become worthless if you don't have energy and enthusiasm to implement them. A powerful health programme is a must for any leader who wishes to bring world transformation. But a powerful health programme becomes useless if you do not implement it. First few steps are always hardest with aches and pains all over body. But continue the programme with self-determination. You must face and fight out the forces of old habits. But once you continue with the health programme, soon you become addicted to it because of the release of internal endorphin, a powerful and addictive "Feel Good Hormone."

14] Thinking in silence-Get up at least one hour early when others are sleeping. It is an excellent discipline for excellent performance. BK-Rajayoga advices to get up at 4am, the time phase called as Amrut vela. The belief is that our micro-consciousness or microcosm gets immediately connected to Supreme Consciousness during this Brahmi muhurta as there is no impedance from negative thought vibrations of others. A flow of positive thoughts may begin giving innovative but by far the best solutions to a problem you are facing. Single pointed focus of thoughts [Ekagra chitta avastha] is achieved. This shall be experienced in the form of totally relaxed but focussed state of mind and a total relaxation of the body [This is Shavasan described by sage Patanjali 2500 years ago]. Current research in the institutes of Mind Body Medicine in USA has shown that certain rejuvenating neurohormones are secreted from the brain during this phase which maintain health and cure the incurable diseases. Self-reflection creates intensity of clarity and helps you to focus on "Core priorities." Getting up early gives a head start of minimum one hour. Only thing that is required is to get out of your "Comfort zone." Real life begins at the end of the comfort zone. BK-Rajayoga concepts clearly tell this. If you get up at 4am then you are a Raja yogi. The devotees get up at 5am and begin the day by begging for something from the God. The person who gets up at 6am is lazy or Bhogi [enjoyer] and the late riser at 7am or beyond it is a Rogi or an ill or sick person.

15] Robin Sharma about transpersonal relationships

15.1] Ego-Remember ego means erasing God out of your equation. It raises an invisible and insurmountable barrier between two individuals. Ego wants to hear only its voice and only its desire to be fulfilled. It is impossible for ego to forgive others and also does not have ability to ask for forgiveness. Give permission to yourself to be open, straight, truthful and happy. When the **consciousness** in untainted like this then the Happiness Quotient **[HQ]** is taken care of and it remains elevated. Others also reciprocate by being open, real and happy. Just being around you makes them feel safe and great. They begin to relax and open up. Mutual trust grows and amazing things begin to happen. BK-concepts tell that with regular meditation all of these effects start happening because of the soul starts sending powerfully positive vibrations in the surrounding.

15.2] Stay firmly committed to your mission, values and to the fullest expression of the inner giant, the spiritualist mind which normally lies dormant. BK-Rajayoga awakens this giant which is full of power, wisdom and experience of last innumerable births and lifetimes. This unshakable belief and faith in your own potential shall not allow tohave any doubts when people criticize you, condemn you or find faults with your thinking. The trick is to believe in your **own self** when nobody is willing to believe you. You shall meet great resistance and criticism. People around you shall discourage you. Criticism is the weapon of weak persons to protect themselves from leaving their "Comfort zone." Raw drive and initiative always gets mocked ,ridiculed and insulted. Some shall harass you. **Jealousy** is a tribute that mediocrity always pays to a genius. Remember one never goes wrong while doing right. BK-Rajayoga gives such mind empowerment that **self-doubt** never arises.

15.3] Maintain "**Architecture of integrity.**" Pristine name and fame always maintains impeccably ethical and moral behaviour. One unethical bad act **[vikarma]** in the moment of weakness makes one repent for whole of lifetime. Integrity in face of most adverse situations always leads to beautiful rewards. BK-Rajayoga ensures perpetual connection with the Supreme powerhouse and thus prevents us from falling in "**Money traps**" or "**Honey traps**" or any momentary weakness.

15.4] Let your video be in sync with your audio. BK-Rajayoga commands that there should not be any difference between your words and corresponding act **[Karma]**. Be a truthful and inspirational communicator. Speak with candour and forthrightness. Never hold back or speak in generalization. Then the people shall know that they shall always get a straight talk from you. Be first to speak **the truth**. Truth is very powerful and it has an uncanny habit of springing up at the most unexpected time. In this way, problems shall fester if you do not stick to reality. **Plastic slogan mongering** and false assurances makes the misunderstanding to grow. Such communication which tries to hide the real situation makes the people to lose trust in you.

15.5] Being candid and straight forward does not mean that you should be rude. Whatever you want to communicate, you say it with humility, respect and **sweetness**. BK-Rajayoga teaches you to be always polite and extremely sweet even with your strongest critic, enemy or opponent. Employ supporting, calming, encouraging and positive words. People always remember something hurtful that was said to them. Your words should activate and motivate. They should make **the other person happy** about himself. The people shall then support you under most stressful circumstances. Tough talk never brings good results.

15.6] Your words can influence your own state of mind and health. The words are nothing but an act that results from your thoughts. Latest medical science called **Psycho-neuro-immunology** or Mind Body Medicine has proved that the negative thoughts are powerful weapons of self-destruction. Positive thoughts and words are wonderful instruments for magical cure and healing. Bad mouthing reveals your negative points. Focus on the best and neglect the rest. Shift from chaotic complexity to **elegant simplicity**. Dr. Massaru Emoto's **water crystallography** is quite an eye opener in this regard. Water in glass was bombarded with words of hate, anger, jealousy, hatred, suspicion, discouragement, humiliation or repulsion. The water crystals on examination showed ferocious, deranged, distorted or disorganized structures on each occasion. On the contrary, when words of encouragement, hope, praise, joy, appreciation or expressing firm belief and faith were used, the water crystals showed beautifully arranged kaleidoscopic patterns. This research is quite important as about 80 per cent of our body mass is formed by water. Unfortunately, modern medical science, without even the benefit of investigating effect on health, has dismissed the valuable work of Dr. Emoto as **pseudoscience**.

15.7] INNER DISCIPLINE WITH SELF-AWARENESS-
These two ingredients along with swift execution helps you to remain ahead of everybody, always keep alive your PMF-Pimary Motivational Factor for remaining ahead of others all the time. Appropriate and quick decision making is a rare quality. Sometimes the success is not about taking a right decision. It is more about **making some decision**. Avoiding to decide is also a decision. Standing frozen and blind amidst a catastrophe is also a decision. But these are wrong decisions from a shell shocked mind. BK-Rajayoga practice helps you to keep calm and allows finding effective and best solutions by way of out of box thinking. **Silenced Scientist Mind** brings such capabilities. Remember that letting your doubts and fear take hold of you makes you feel uncomfortable for a life time. Stop worrying about things you cannot control. Identify and focus on an area on which you have a control .Then move ahead.

Chapter 2: Brahma Kumaris Rajayoga – A God Given Mantra for Health and Success

The principles of success lucidly given by Robin Sharma are difficult when one actually tries to implement them in modern times. The main reason is the lack of will power or self –determination [**mano-nigrah**]. The devil or Shaitan is most powerful in the present era called Iron Age. Lust anger, greed, ego, attachment, jealousy, hatred, repulsion and doubts are the age old weapons of the devil. The advanced armoury includes stress, tension, anxiety, worry, fear and frustration. Frustration in advanced stages becomes **Depression** and in worst cases, a **Burn Out**. No wonder that ancient Indian scriptures describe that Iron Age or kali yug is an era of mass confusion and hallucination [**Bhrushta. mati**]. Five thousand years old Bhagavad Gita describes a mythological battle in which Mahaveer Arjuna develops all the signs and symptoms of acute depression. Lord Krishna's quick fix psychotherapy makes Arjuna battle worthy. BK-concepts tell that the whole description of an action on a battlefield sounds illogical and irrational. In fact we in modern age represent the depressed and frustrated **Arjuna**. Then incorporeal Supreme Father , Supreme Teacher and Supreme Sadgatidata appears on planet earth and imparts lifesaving and mind-saving supreme knowledge about a novel technique of mind empowerment through a human conduit. This human conduit is then known as Brahma Baba who imparts celestial knowledge to whole of the mankind. **The easy technique for extremely busy people** of modern times is BK-Rajayoga which in reality is a scientific Self-Management Leadership Programme [**SML**]. Regular practice awakens the giant within you who has tremendous power, experience and wisdom. This is in fact **self-realization** which is the aim of the spiritual practices. BK-Rajayoga tells you how you could achieve this miracle even while you are in **Grihasthashram** fulfilling both mundane materialistic gains as well as **spiritual evolution**. You do not have to go Himalaya like sages. It is **Nivrutti Marg** [Path of a sanyasi]. BK-Rajayoga teaches you a novel **Pravrutti marg** [active spiritual evolution in the face of temptations and attractions]. Self-realization is the first step to God realization. In last twenty one years have achieved God realization like the millions of Brahma Kumars

[Bachelors] and **adhar Kumars** [married person]. The **divine Muralis** read in 11500 centres in 140 countries gives self-experience of having a talk with God and receiving direction from Him. Even a super intelligent person even if he tries his best cannot recite whole of Murali verbatim. It is an exhilarating experience that THE ONE AND ONLY ONE whom whole of the world is searching, comes daily to a BK-Centre and talks personally to each of those who are present. This belief has come from the knowledge that only a few specific sentences from the Murali touch the heart of each and every person. These are actually **celestial directions** from the Supreme consciousness the person for showing his weaknesses and suggestions for improvement. This spiritual effort brings about a gradual but definite self-empowerment. **BK-R.E.R.F.**[Rajayoga Education and Research Foundation] and its medical and S.P.A.R.C. wings have certain novel instruments which could demonstrate the experiential **transcendental stages** of meditation. The book-**"Spiritual Medicine for modern lifestyle diseases, April 2018** gives lucid description of these instruments.

BK-RAJAYOGA AS HIGHWAY TO HEALTH AND SUCCESS

Essential components

1] A free of cost foundation course available in all 11500 centres in 140 countries.

2] Getting up at amrit vela[brahma muhurta] for meditation for one hour [Long meditation].

3] Traffic control-every hour for **just one minute** if done regularly does not allow the negative and waste thoughts to accumulate in the mind.

4] Daily attendance at the nearest BK-centre for listening to celestial Murali. **Phone number** 09999333555/666 gives the address and phone number of the nearest centre.

5] No TV or newspaper reading or any discussion about mundane affairs at least half an hour before going to sleep. A short meditation for 15 minutes is prescribed before going to sleep for cleaning out the negative and the waste that has accumulated in mind. This facilitates getting a childlike deep rejuvenating sleep. **Cyber scan and HRI-**Heartfelt Resonance Imaging during this meditation helps to identify the most **predominant thought** prevailing in your mind. If it is negative, it could be removed by appropriate autosuggestions and visualization. These two techniques in psychotherapy are most powerful as they bring about a positive transformation of the mind-set [**Vrutti**] within 21 days. Neuroscience has confirmed this concept. If a single positive thought is repeated daily for most of the time per day, then it gets embedded in the psyche as a seed. This seed undergoes immediate sprouting under appropriate adverse situation and does not allow one to lose his calm. Hence BK-Rajayoga could give permanent liberation from the addiction in its De-addiction Programme in Maharashtra in eight districts. Author has participated in the programme in Wardha District.

6] **Divine Garbh Sanskar** [DGS] [Dr. Shubhada Neel 09820676002] is yet another project in Maharashtra which is ensuring a progeny of extremely jovial and intelligent children who have a novel spiritual equilibrium. The granddaughter of **Padmashree Dr. Lahane** the charismatic Dean of the world famous Sir J J Hospital, Mumbai and the author's granddaughter are the products of Divine Garbh Sanskar.

BK-SPIRITUAL CONCEPTS-

Author personally believes that **Islam** and **Vedas** are the only two real scriptures which teach the **art of living.** Undivided Bharat probably had only these two major religions [**Dharma**]. Religions over time decayed into ritualism, dogmatism and fanaticism. The terrorism is final step in degradation of the soul. Bhagawad Gita is five thousand years old. Holy Quran is 1400 years old. But this scripture came into existence in a span of 25 years; some part of it was written during a time/phase which was full of war and turbulence. Holy Quran in the times of peace gives an entirely different Message from The One and The Only One. Human race had to survive in the times of war. Even **Mohammad Paigamber**, the greatest and the last Messiah, had to fight in war and the miracle was that he won.

I am amazed by the similarity between the Messages given by Mohammad Paigamber and those given by **Dada Lekhraj**, an internationally renowned and very rich diamond merchant in Pakistan. Both Messiah received Celestial Message through mystical experiences. As hallucinations [Bhrum] and the mystical experience [sakashtkars] occur in the same area of brain, doctors find it difficult to believe and have faith in Brahma Kumaris concepts. The BK-concepts were not in the form of a book. One receives knowledge from the Supreme Soul when one attends the **Murali class** regularly. Now the set of books called **Avyakta Muralis** from year 1970 to 1985 are available. Self-study [**swadhyaya**] of this book gives a clear understanding in depth.

WHY PEOPLE SHUN BRAHMA KUMARIS RAJAYOGA?

1] The divine guidelines demand observance of strict celibacy even in thoughts, consumption of vegetarian food, a definite charter of Dos and Don'ts Dos which are same as Yama and niyama in Patanjali sutra. All of this becomes an essential part of daily routine. Forsaking the different pleasures of modern life becomes a great burden to the modern man who is habituated to them. But the practice of mere three months of BK-Rajayoga brings about radical transformation. Then the impossible becomes I am possible. This is the main reason why de-addiction by BK-Rajayoga is permanent.

2] Scientism-This could be labelled as mental affliction in which a person refuses to believe and have faith in something unless it has been proved by science. The extraordinary dominance of Scientist Mind in dominant brain hemisphere is responsible for this trait. In extreme cases the Scientist Mind may demand DNA proof from the parents to believe that they are its parents. Padmabhushan Dr. R.D. Lele sir, my favourite teacher refuses to believe in the existence of soul and God until the Neutrino research in NOL-Neutrino Observatory laboratory in Bengaluru gets completed. Reverently I asked him when this research is likely to get completed. The answer from this 91 years old genius was in 2050. Here I felt my favourite teacher is somewhat lacking in wisdom or **Vivek** or an ability to differentiate between right and wrong.

3] Both Islamic derived given by tenets and the BK-concepts called as Shrimat were derived through mystical experiences the incorporeal God. As both mystical experiences and hallucinations occur in the same area of cerebral cortex, doctors immediately dismiss them as hallucinations.

4] God, soul, acupressure points or acupuncture points and seven energy chakras are metaphysical in nature. So they could be experienced but science may not be able to prove their existence. The experiences and mystical experiences happen only when person has belief and faith. The spiritual Mind or subconscious mind functions on belief and faith. So a firm and unshakable belief activates this Inner Giant which in turns brings about miracles. An Experience or an event that could not be explained by science becomes a miracle. **BK Dr. Satish Gupta,** an eminent cardiologist in Apollo hospital, Delhi resigned when he realized that the interventions he has been a advising has completely destroyed several thousands of families financially. His study of BK-Rajayoga giving **cent per cent removal of blocks in heart vessels** within three to six months is a miracle. It got published in Indian Heart Journal **in 2011.** American Heart Journal refused to publish it because of the pressures from drug mafia. American health commerce just can't afford that Indians may get well by regular asana, pranayama and BK-Rajayoga.

5] Belief and faith are two very powerful primary motivational factors [**PMF**] apart from love. Several scientific papers have appeared in medical journals in which **placebos** [non-medicinal substances] were proved to be 70 to 300 times more effective than the drug itself. This resulted in closure of several drug manufacturing companies in USA as the FDA in USA is very strict. If a placebo is 30 or more times effective than the drug, then use of that drug is immediately discontinued. **R.E.R.F.**-Rajayoga Education and Research Foundation and its **SPARC** wing and Medical wing have certain novel

instruments that could demonstrate the deep meditation experience. But these instruments require **scientific validation** by a systematic multicentric research in recognised Medical research institutes. The greatest hurdle in this task is that modern medical science immediately labels such alternative therapies as **Pseudoscience**. Diploma in **Radionics or Vibrionics** is regularly issued through several institutes in USA. But FDA in USA calls it as pseudoscience. **Dr. Abraham** MD who is the pioneer of Radionics was given a dubious degree of **Dean of faculty of quackery** by his jealous compatriots in a public function. But contrary to all expectations the clinical practice of Dr. Abraham rose several hundred fold after this event.

SECRET OF SUCCESS BY BK-RAJAYOGA

1] Clear, calm and very stable mind by BK-Rajayoga-

Roger Sperry, a Physiologist in 1970 got noble prize for his novel concept of one brain and two minds. Edward De Bonois's twin hemisphere theory is proved by Sperry concept. Though there is a lot of talk about the Mind, Westerners do not know the precise definition of the mind. The main reason is that the **concept of consciousness** is unknown in Western world. Mind is the virtual screen formed by a manifestation of consciousness in the soul or Atman. The thoughts, emotions and desires form as transient waves on this virtual screen. When any one thought is repeated often, then it results in appropriate karma [act]. Repetition of the bad act in spite of the loud protest by the subconscious mind, or **inner voice**, it becomes a habit. A habit is difficult to remove because you remove H, Abit remains. You remove A, a Bit remains. Finally remove B, it remains. The only remedy is to remove **I or ego**. Then the T or transformation happens. BK-Rajayoga makes it very easy to remove bad habits and to rewrite the corrupted CD of mind with positive thoughts.

2] **Scientist mind** in the dominant brain hemisphere is logical, analytical and judgemental. It is also **a seat of negative** thoughts, emotions and desires. Intelligent mind is an agile mind like a monkey. It cannot focus properly. Innumerable thoughts in a day, especially the negative ones, tire the mind. E.E.G.[electroencephalogram] shows **fast beta waves** during this mental turmoil. BK-Rajayoga silences this mind and brings out the spiritualist mind. Once the functioning is taken over by subconscious mind, everything becomes quick, accurate, easy and automatic. Remember what happens when one is learning car driving. Multiple instructions from the scientist mind confuse you. In consequence you press accelerator instead of the break. Once car driving has been learnt, the spiritualist mind takes over making everything easy and automatic. **Two seconds snap judgements** about a person or a problem always turn out to be accurate. This is because the vast data of experiences of last several births helps to take a quick but most accurate decision. **Silence of mind** is a very powerful state. **Mirror neurons** receive vibrations as signals from the other person and give a quick, accurate judgement about the other person even when not a single word has been spoken. This faculty is tremendously improved by regular practice of BK-Rajayoga. Many a **divorces** in the modern times shall be avoided if the ladies use this faculty for assessing their life partners. EEG shows maximum Right and Left brain coherence in the phase of silence. This is the foundation for intuition, hut feeling or sixth sense and Emotional Intelligence [EQ] or empathy.

3] Out of Box thinking or Lateral thinking-

The quietening of scientist mind helps the microcosm or spiritualist mind to establish a connection with cosmic Google. A sudden flow of thoughts or inspirations come to the mind as if from the cosmos which give innovative solutions to the problem one is facing. Or it may strengthen your belief and faith in a concept for going **an extra mile** to achieve the set goal. When you have exhausted all of your resources and concepts, a time comes when you have to decide about going an extra mile. If decision is correct then magnificent results happen. If decision is wrong then whole effort is lost. Please remember famous **Benzene ring** was discovered while dreaming. Famous painter **Salvatore Dali** used to keep one spoon in his hand and a tin plate below while going to sleep. No sooner the **REM** [Rapid Eye movements] sleep starts, innovative ideas were seen in dreams. Salvatore then used to wake up and draw the designs which he had seen in his dream in REM sleep. The resultant paintings were out of the world.

4] Focus –

Ekagra chitta avastha described by sage Patanjali 2500 years ago is today known as **"The Zone"**, a term coined by **Dr. Herbert Benson**, an American cardiologist. He gave the name of BRR-Biological Relaxation Response to Shavasan described by Patanjali. **Gavaskar** in Port of Spain scored two hundred runs in face of the ferocious attack by West Indian bowlers. This was when batsman did not use helmets and a casualty has happened in the form of Nari Contractor, the opening Indian batsman, getting a head injury. When asked how he managed this courage, Sunil Gavaskar simply answered-"I was in the zone. I saw nothing else but the ball."

5] S.W.O.T. analysis-
When the mindfulness mediation like BK-Rajayoga begins, all the deficiencies and weakness residing in the Self or Atman come to the surface. Appropriate autosuggestions and visualization help to remove these weaknesses.

As the meditative experience deepens one becomes aware about the strengths that are inherent in each soul. Specific autosuggestions and visualization help to give a further strength to the inherent qualities of the soul.

Usually opportunities come as a great threat to comfort zone. So we tend to leave them and forced to repent later. The opportunities always knock only once.

Threats usually come in the garb of wonderful opportunities. We tend to jump at them and repent later.

A calm, clear experienced and powerful Spiritualist Mind helps **to differentiate** accurately between opportunity and threat. Thus there is always success and no repentance.

6] Strict adherence to morals and ethics

BK-Rajayoga empowers mind to such an extent that momentary weaknesses do not happen. The person becomes resistant to pressures, enticements, criticism attractions and temptations. He remains firmly committed to morals and ethics in life.

7] The technique of BK-Rajayoga involves awakening the lost memory about the **self or atman** and its inherent divine qualities namely **peaceful, loveful, blissful, pure and powerful.** Repeated autosuggestions about each divine quality or virtue and concomitant visualization in meditation strengthens and potentiates each quality. As a result of this **self-empowerment** any tough situation does not pose any problem for the individual. He remains confident that come what may he shall find the best solution to the problem. This is the state of **spiritual equilibrium** [Sthitpragnya avastha of consciousness. Dadi Janaki, the international Head of this **global N.G.O.** with six peace awards and **consultative status in U.N.O.** has been certified to have achieved this state and that she has the most stable mind in the whole world.

8] **Ken Wilber** talks about Atman to Atman transpersonal human transactions in his book of transpersonal psychology for effective human resource development and management. Today USA has a huge institute of Ken Wilber's transpersonal psychology. **BK-Rajayoga** talks about the same Atman to Atman transactions at higher level of consciousness which always ensure success.

BK-RAJAYOGA, HEALTH AND IMPOSSIBLE CURES

Mind Body Medicine is the latest and the most advanced branch of modern medicine. Dr. Herbert Benson, an American cardiologist, founded the first **institute of Mind Body Medicine** in year 1970. He received the accolade of Sir because of his novel research in most innovative branch of medicine. He coined two famous terms-BRR-Biological Relaxation Response and The zone. This is the modern and scientifically accepted nomenclature for **Shavasan** and **Ekagra chitta** avastha by the sage Patanjali about 2500 years ago. Kriya yog of Patanjali has six main components-Yama, Niyama, Asana, Pranayama, Dhyan, Dharana if practiced diligently result in **Moksha** or emancipation from the diseases and ageing. Wit, vitality, vigour and vision are preserved till last breath and the death is as easy as described in **Mahamrutunjaya Mantra**. Dhyan gives mind empowerment and then Dharana means inculcating the divine qualities in one's own nature [**Vrutti**] becomes very easy. Dr. Richard Davidson, Professor and Head of Psychiatry division in Wisconsin University, USA, in 2003 baptized Dhyan and Dharana as **Mindfulness Meditation**. Since he worked with Buddhist form of meditation called as **Vipassana**, Mindfulness meditation became synonymous with the Buddhist form of meditation. **Mindfulness** means such power of mind that one could focus on any one positive thought [sankalpa] for any length of time whenever one desires in matter of seconds. BK-Rajayoga ensures this power of mind if practiced diligently and daily without interruptions

for five years or more. A practitioner starts getting positive strokes from the Supreme Consciousness **within ten days to three months**. Further positive experiences and outcomes go on strengthening the belief and faith to an unshakable level. This is the most important goal to achieve. The person then gets **Vacha siddhi** [spoken words become a reality] and **Sankalpa siddhi** [Thought becomes a reality]. Author after a practice of nearly ten years is having the experiences of such miraculous powers.

The process of mindfulness is commonly confused with mental relaxation. **Dr. Herbert Benson** has proved that if you chant Om Om or One One repeatedly it gives a total physical and mental relaxation. But there is no **transformation** of satanic traits into divine traits. Two types of meditations have been described on the basis of this finding

1] **Concentrative** and relaxation oriented meditations and

2] **Mindfulness** or Transformation oriented meditations. BK-Rajayoga is an evidence based Mindfulness meditation which is under extensive research by the Medical wing of Brahma kumaris and by Psychiatry, Medicine and Cardiology departments of world famous **Sir J J Hospital and research Institute at Mumbai. Padmashree Dr. T.P. Lahane** an internationally renowned ophthalmologist whose name is in the **Guinness records** for maximum number of cataract surgeries brought a novel **chemiluminiscence** instrument for Biochemistry Department. This instrument could process 1800 blood samples in an hour. So whole of the load of investigations could be finished within 4 hours. In addition it has an attachment called Verna. This diverts the half the drop of blood to a processor used for estimating **Stress hormones** and **neurohormones**. Thus this instrument has become most important piece of procurement for a **systematic study of deep meditative experiences**. BK medical wing also has five novel instruments for this very purpose. The details are given in the Book-"Spiritual Medicine for modern lifestyle diseases, April 2018" available with the medical wing of Brahma kumaris and now with First Step Publishers.

How the health benefits by BK-Rajayoga are achieved?

Regular practice gives BRR and the zone or Single pointed laser beam focus of positive thoughts in a matter of few seconds. In this state a miraculous **internal equilibrium** or balance of all the physiological and biochemical process inside the body is achieved through several mechanisms

1] Dangerous **Cerebral** genes revealed in **Allen's brain map** have given birth to a branch of Mind Body Medicine called as **Neurogenetics**. Cerebral genes remain quiet in the blissful, peaceful and powerful state of mind. But stress, anxiety, worry, fear, frustration or doubts activate them to release certain powerful enzymes. These in turn activate the disease producing somatic genes and cancer genes called as **oncogenes**. Each oncogene is responsible a particular type of cancer. Hence in some cases **Polyoma** or multiple types of cancers could happen because of the presence of more than 200 oncogens presence in the body. Now, what decides that some people have allergies, others have heart attacks or Diabetes or Parkinsonism or dreadful or mild cancers depends on the laws of **karma theory** given in Bhagavad Gita. Sins or **Kufra** or bad acts [Vikarma] in past life result in accumulation of bad Karmic Load. This results in Bhog or pain and sufferings in life. Bhog is of four types-Of the mind [Mana], of the people [Jana], of body [Tana] or Wealth [dhan] or a combination of all the four types of Bhog. When I was on the **path of Bhakti** and in ISKCON , I knew that I could shed the bad karmic load by suffering only. BK-Rajayoga from Supreme Consciousness assured that you could **burn out your bad karmic Load** by intense or volcanic meditation [**Jwalamukhi Yaad**]. This dictum got proved by personal experiential evidence of emancipation from seven incurable diseases. The dictum in BK-Rajayoga and also in Mind Body Medicine is that **"Incurable means whose cure lies within."**

2] Rejuvenating and recharging neurohormones released from brain during mindfulness state bring about conquest of grey hair, of dim vision [cataract], of ageing and of diseases.

2.1] Encephalin-restores the internal balance of ions, lipids and sugar. This derangement is the most important cause of High B.P., Heart attacks and Diabetes. It also causes "A reverse transport of cholesterol" from the plaques in heart vessels. This probably was the reason for the miraculous CAD-regression [Coronary artery disease] by BK Rajayoga in the innovative research by BK Dr. Satish Gupta at Mount Ab Global Hospital.

2.2] Endorphin-This is endogenous morphine like substance which is powerful pain reliever and mood elevator. So the ever blissful state described in ancient Indian scriptures has become a scientific reality today. In **end stage cancer patients,** the intense pain is not relieved by any known pain killer. But the practitioners of BK-Rajayoga seem to bear the pain without any obvious anguish. Endogenous endorphin may be the reason. Unfortunately modern medicine dismisses all such claims **as quackery** without doing any systematic research in this area.

2.3] Melatonin-This miraculous agent is secreted by pineal gland which today is known as **God's spot** or Third eye or Spiritual eye as doctors now believe that the soul or Atman resides in pineal gland. This gland embedded in brain tissue and surrounded by total darkness has an internal structure like the human eye. It has all the machinery to process photons or light energy particles. All of ancient philosophies believe that the pineal gland is the **God's antenna** for catching cosmic signals. It is possible that the pineal gland may be quite large in size in all the Messengers of God. It is possible that cosmic vibrations are converted into photons and then deciphered by pineal gland. Melatonin governs the **sleep wake cycle and circadian biorhythms**. Today melatonin tablets are available for preventing **jet lag**. But we as yet do not know long term side effects of prolonged usage of these tablets. Melatonin is also a powerful **immune-modulator** and anti-cancer agent. It is one of the **Biomarkers** for detecting cancer.

Pineal gland calcification is a precursor of impending death. High levels of **fluorides** in drinking water, use of fluoride pastes and EMR [Electromagnetic radiations] from excessive mobile use promote early calcification of the pineal gland. Consuming three or four litres of **water per day** and plenty of **leafy vegetables** in diet prevent pineal gland calcification. The acid test that indicates that enough water is consumed is getting crystal clear water like urine all the time.

2.4] BDNF-Brain Derived Neurotropic Factor [2003] gives the miracle of **neurogenesis** i.e. nerve cell multiplication. This could be preventing senility. Senile dementia, Alzheimer related dementias and alcohol related psychosis. Most of the current anti-depressants today act by promoting increases in BDNF and hence they could be safely taken over for almost a life time. **Memory enhancement** and Ekpathy, Dwipathy or Tripathy could become scientific realities. Vedas were taught verbally without any books. Persons had the mental sharpness to remember whole of what has been heard by listening once, twice or thrice. Today we are unable to use the full power of our brain and mind. **Geniuses use only 5 per cent** of the brain power. **Stereotaxic technique** shows that ninety per cent of our brains consist of a **silent area**. Is this the area where our spiritualist mind resides?

2.5] SCAF-Stem Cell Activation Factor-Each tissue in our bodies harbours some totipotential cells which could convert themselves into any form of the tissue. For example brain tissue, heart muscle or knee cartilage. SCAF stimulates the stem cells in the damaged area and bring about complete rejuvenation by regeneration of the damaged tissues. **Cytotrone therapy** [Dr. Vasishth Mumbai phone 09900548375] works on this principle. Low intensity energy waves stimulate cartilage formation and complete cure of the knee pain happens without knee surgery. This therapy is available at Bengaluru with a very pious **Dr. G. S. Nayar [phone number 09741118867]**. High intensity waves are used for destroying the deep seated cancer metastases. Five cases of fatal **cardiomyopathy** type b and three cases of incurable **macular degeneration** have been cured by Mindfulness programme.

Another miraculous example of the role of **Energy medicine** in cure is the **Korean spiral therapy** practiced by Dr. Jatin Chaudhari at Delhi [phone number 09811286852]. Famous Tennis star Sania Mirza could play again because of this acupuncture therapy. She underwent an operation in USA. Australian Physiotherapist announced that she is fit to play. But after the first serve only Sania developed intense pain. A second operation was advised. But **cricketer Yuvraj** conveyed the story of his miraculous cure. So Sania, against all medical advice and resistance from family opted for Spiral therapy. She bore the terrible pain of therapy with a very strong will power. The result was for the whole world to see. She went on winning one tournament after another and won highest accolades.

BK-Dr Rahul Lakhotiya, an orthopaedic surgeon from Delhi, now at Shantivan of Brahma Kumaris practices Prolo-ozone therapy for knee pain and back pain.[**0838709555**].

2.6] RMF-Receptor Modulation Factor-This is a unique substance which could convert a dream of disease less and infection less states into reality.

Receptors are the tiny points on the surface of all the cells in the body. There is specific receptor for each hormone, enzyme, microbe, antigen, antibody or haptane or partial antigen. Attachment to the receptor is the first step for giving infection or diseases by stress hormones. RMF inactivates the specific receptor and thus prevents disease or infection from happening. Today the stress born NCDs[Non-infectious Chronic Diseases] like heart attacks, Diabetes, Cancer, Depression, Alzheimer's, Parkinsonism and cancer have risen to alarming proportion. An independent **NCD wing** was opened in the year 2012 in the Directorate of Health Services Maharashtra, to check this alarming rise. The failure is because of only one reason. The modern medical students do not have the current information on Mind Body Medicine which could be precisely called as **Spiritual Medicine**. Proactive Vice Chancellor of MUHS, **Dr. Dileep Mhaisekar** is trying his best to include a short add-on syllabus of spiritual medicine in MBBS course since 2017. His efforts resulted in submitting the recommendations of Dr. Kaundinya Committee to MCI in 2017. But in 2018 MCI got dissolved by a Supreme Court judgement. **Padmabhushan Dr. R.D. Lele**, Dr. Sujal Shah, President of Jain Doctors Federation, Dr. Matcheswalla, renowned Honorary Professor of

Psychiatry at Sir J J Hospital, Mumbai, Padmashree Dr. Alaka Deshpande and Dr. Naras Bhat , Professor of Mind Body Medicine ,Seymore University, USA have sent letters to the Honourable Academic council of MUHS supporting the contention of Dr. Mhaisekar. **As yet there has not been a positive outcome.**

2.7] Sirtuins-These miraculous agents help to delay the ageing process. So the conquest of ageing may not a myth.

3] Cosmic Healing Vibrational Whisper-Modern science does not believe in the existence of body aura, seven energy chakras, acupressure cum acupuncture points and healing vibrations. I personally believe that the modern medicine has put down the mental shutters and refuses to investigate scientifically. So anything that does not fit in the bracket of modern medical science is declared as **pseudoscience**. Energy medicine has provided proof for the existence of Life Force Energy [**Prana**], **Carl Simonton's Psycho-oncology** has proved the miraculous healing power of the mind , **kirlian Body aura photography** proves the existence of body aura and **Faraday cage experiment has** proved that the healing thought vibrations could travel to an infinite distance. Thus curing of an ailment of a patient in England by Third grade Reiki master in India is no more a myth. **Dr. Naras Bhat** in his wonderful **book on reversing cancer, ageing and heart attacks**, talks about a cosmic healing vibrational whisper that traverses through all **energy chakras** – Sahasara at the top. Agya, Vishuddi, Anahat, Manipura, Swadhishthan and Muladhar and provides life force energy to the different tissues of the body. In fact, the term **Healthy means Heal Thy**. Each energy chakra is a distribution point for dispensing Life Force Energy [Pranik Shakti] to a fixed set of tissues and organs. Sahasara chakra possibly represents highest level of pure and powerful consciousness. This may be the precursor to the **Karmateet avastha**. Supreme Father of all souls tells in His Muralis that once the Karmateet avastha is attained, the soul has to leave this body which came into existence because of Vikara. The soul attains the highest state of pure deity like consciousness. **Agya chakra,** the Third eye or Spiritual eye [Divya chakshu] supplies pranik force to tissues in the cranium and face. **Vishuddi chakra** in the neck provides rejuvenation to structures In the neck especially Thyroid and Parathyroid glands. Anahat chakra is the distributor for organs in the thorax. Further distribution is **Manipura** chakra for Gastro –intestinal tract, **Swadhishthan** for Genito-urinary tract and **Muladhar** chakra is for genital tract. BK-Dr. Chandrasekhar's **aura scanner** demonstrates the extent of body aura as well as the blocks in different chakras. The presence of block correlated beautifully with the ailments of the persons in an experiment I had witnessed at BK-Centre, Nagpur. BK-Dr. Chandrasekhar then proceeded to charge the water in a glass after brief BK-Rajayoga Meditation. When this charged water was given to the persons with ailments, the blocks in the energy chakra disappeared. Modern Medicine needs to investigate such phenomena so that the **quackery** could be differentiated from real health benefit. Obvious deduction from the observation is that a cosmic energy was transferred to water in the glass by brief meditation. But could it be proved by advanced scientific experiments?

Carl Simonton's institute of **Psycho-oncology**, USA, harnesses the immense healing power of mind by a mindfulness programme. The persons who diligently followed the instructions became totally cancer free. **Bernie Siegel** called them **EcaP** Exceptional cancer patients. Survival of the patients was found to double.

4] Psycho-neuro-immunology [PNI]-This branch of Mind Body Medicine investigates the deleterious effects of the omnipresent and omnipotent stress on brain, heart and endocrines.

4.1] T-Lymphocyte or Thymic Lymphocyte development-Normal pathway is **Th-1 pathway** which is the course when the mind is happy and peaceful. Th-1 immune response potentiates the Tumour Necrosis Factor [**TNF**] and gives rise to a fibrocaseous tissue response in an effort to limit the spread of infection in Tuberculosis. Interferon; a universal anti-viral agent in human blood becomes potentiated giving sizeable immunity to viral infections. Vaccines and toxoids give powerful immunity. On the other hand when the mind is full of stress, **Th-2 immune response** happens. The infection assumes dangerous wide spread form of Tuberculosis called as Miliary Tuberculosis. Interferons diminished in their anti-viral effect. Anti-viral immunity gets diminished. The vaccines and toxoids may not give protective effect.

4.2] Agile brain giving fast beta waves in EEG [Electroencephalogram] tires the mind and the individual. Accumulation of lactic acid happens in the muscles giving tiredness. **Chronic Fatigue**

Syndrome [CFS] has become common today especially in Western countries. Various viruses have been implicated. But these may only be incidental associations and not real causative agents. Real cause may lie in the mind. **BK-Rajayoga** gives rapid disappearance of lactic acid from the muscles and transforms fast beta waves into slower alpha waves initially. On prolonged meditation, the practitioner may demonstrate extremely slow **delta waves** of deep sleep. A complete rejuvenation may happen. Hence in BK-parlance meditation is often known as **battery charging**. Cosmic energy in addition to internal mechanisms results in recharging and rejuvenation.

4.3] the power of giving-Philanthropy is the greatest mood elevator. But in the present era called Iron Age, a man has developed a passion of receiving and never giving. Actually a human being or BMSO-Body Mind Soul Organism has an inbuilt mechanism which promotes giving and philanthropy. Human brain is equipped with a **Reward Centre, a Punishment Centre** and a **reverberating circuit**. Whenever a human being donates [daan] or does some good karma[Act] he feels extremely happy because of the activation of Reward Centre and the release of Feel Good

Hormones. This happy state of mind is maintained for a long time due to reverberating circuit. On the contrary whenever a man commits a sin or bad karma[Vikarma] Punishment centre get activated releasing harmful stress hormones giving rise to various stress associated diseases eventually. This is how the bad karma catches out with the erring human being. This damaging effect remains for a very long time because of Reverberating circuit. Hence BK-Rajayoga stresses to become a **Devata or a giver** instead of a levata or receiver.

TAKE HOME MESSAGE

1] Watch TV channel **peace of mind** which runs for 4 hours on all days. **BK-Shivani** tells in her beautiful and unique style how and why to apply the God given spiritual concepts of Brahma Kumaris from the present moment in all the spheres of life. Health, Happiness, harmony, peace, prosperity and success in life become guaranteed.

2] Visit nearest BK-centre for a free of cost foundation course. There are 11500 BK-centres in 140 countries.

3] Phone 0999933555 or 09999333666 for the knowing the nearest BK-centre.

4] Make Amrut vela meditation, traffic control and half an meditation before sleep an essential part of your daily routine [**Dincharya**]. If you set your Daily routine in accordance with BK-Rajayoga principles, you shall never get upset in life.

5] Proceed with total trusting surrender, belief and faith. All of your doubts, diseases and problems shall disappear miraculously within three months.

APPENDIX – I

Total Health Programme [T.H.P.] <u>Free of Cost</u>
Spiritual Health Clinic
Lecture Hall, St. George Hospital, Near C.S.T., Mumbai

AIMS- [BK-COLABA CENTRE]
1. MY SOCIETY, A HAPPY AND HEALTHY SOCIETY.
2. MY HOSPITAL, ADDICTION FREE HOSPITAL

Components of Total Health Programme [09-01-2015]
1. Current Research in Mind Body Medicine - Dr. Dilip V. Kaundinya MD
2. Sukshma Yogabhyas -
3. Pranayama-
4. Scientific BK-Rajayoga- Mindfulness Based Stress Reduction Programme- [R-MBSRP]-
5. Pranayama Motivated Defecation [P.M.D.] – discussed in Appendix-2.

PREAMBLE-
Warning- All type of **asana** and **Shuddhi Kriya** must be performed under the supervision of a **trained yoga teacher** until one gets proficient.

Diet- Yogic Satvik vegetarian food though not mandatory, is helpful in attaining the higher spiritual levels quickly. One must remember that the journey of the spiritual path is long and there are **eight levels of Samadhi in spiritual elevation** and evolution.

Non-vegetarian diet gives shortening of telomeres and early ageing. A homemade Maharashtrian thali is the most balanced diet amongst various choices available. **Padmabhushan Dr. R.D. Lele** has described various **anti-oxidants and immune modulators** in this vegetarian diet in his wonderful book- Ayurveda and modern medicine, published by **Bharatiya Vidya Bhavan, Mumbai, 2001.**

Garlic and onion in food are Tamasik i.e. they generate laziness and sluggishness of mind. Author has experimented and discovered that the Total Relaxation Response of Mind and Body [Biological Relaxation Response, BRR and the Zone, [Ekagra Chitta avastha] is delayed while meditating when such diet or stale food is ingested. Anything that is not prepared freshly or stored in a refrigerator is considered as stale in Yogism.

2.1] It is **customary but not mandatory** to begin Yogic practices by chanting a Mantra.

A] **Sarve sukhinaha santu, Sarve santu niramaya, Sarve bhadrani paschyantu, - maa pasche dukh makpunyat.**

Let all the divine persons be happy and disease free. Even the lowest of animals may be protected for their welfare. If we do not give pain to others, the pain and suffering shall never come our way.

OR

B] Aum chanting - Laghu Omkar and Dirgh Omkar

OR

C] **Gayatri mantra** may be recited for 11 times with **proper phonetics** [vaikhari], Upanshu [mumbling tones or 3] by silently chanting. Gayatri mantra is a **Beej mantra**. That means though a proper phonetics is essential for maximum benefit, a practitioner **may begin chanting in any way**. Over a period of time Divine Grace **[Insha Allah]** gradually brings an improvement to the proper level of pronunciation. Author has experienced this phenomenon. Gayatri Mantra is said to potentiate power of differentiation between right and wrong or Vivek. [Buddhi shuddhak]. **Buddhi or wisdom is different from intelligence.** Intelligence is an ability to learn the skills of livelihood quickly. Wisdom is the ability of the person to use his God given intellect properly in accordance with the **eternal laws of morals and ethics.**

An unpublished study tells that the **basal life force energy [Prana]** that exists in and around us is at the level of **2-3 photons** [Light energy particles]. With regular chanting the energy levels may raise upto 5 photon units. A human being can never progress to seven or eight photon level or the level of **the 8th Sun**. Aditya is the first Sun.

2.2] **Sukshma Yogabhyas** includes training in some simple yogic postures for protecting your neck, shoulder, lower back, knees and ankles and maintaining them in a resilient state throughout life.. Annamaya Kosh is made free of impurities. Deep abdominal breathing technique, a cyber-scan with Heartfelt Resonant imaging [HRI] is done prior to the Kriya.

1] Calana Kriya- Loosening practices:- This Kriya help to improve micro-circulation.
A] Neck bending, rotation and twisting
B] Kati Shakti vikasak [Trunk movement]
C] Knee movements
D] **Simple yogic postures [Yogasana]** which could be done at any age. Thus this Sukshma Yogabhyas becomes useful for Geriatric patients and could be implemented in various Geriatric O.P.D.s

Eg. **Tadasana, Vakrasana, Ardha chakrasana, Trikonasana, Ardhaustrasana,** [in supine posture]:- Pavan muktasana, Sarvangasana, Halasan and

Shavasana **[Relaxing posture]**. These yogic postures are performed in prone posture]:- Bhujangasana, Shalabhasana, Naukasana and Makarasana **[relaxing posture]**. Optional- Uttan tadasana and Vishnu shayyasana

2] **Shuddhi Kriya-** Jala neti, Sinha Mudra, Ashwini Mudra [prevents piles and prolapse of rectum] should be done daily
Jal dhoti should be done daily for one month. Later it should be done on every first day and fifteenth day of each month.
Advanced Yogabhyas includes 1] pada hastasana,2] Bhadrasana3] Ardha matsyendrasana,4] Dhunurasana 5]Matsyasana 6]Pachimotanasana and 7] nauli

2.3] **Pranayama-** Eight types of Pranayama exist. Nadi Shuddhi Pranayama is the simplest. If performed along with Jal Neti and Jal Dhoti is a sure cure for asthma and allergies.
Prana means life or oxygen. Ayama means control. This process ensures **maximization of the use of oxygen** that is inhaled.

A] Anulom-vilom or nadi Shuddhi Pranayam B] Kapalbhati 3] Bhramari 4] Bhasarika, 5] Ujjayi 6] Agnisaar 7] Uddiyan bandha 8] Pranayam proper with fixed durations in set proportions for Rechaka [exhalation], Poorak [inhalation-2, Antar Kumbhak[Holding breath after Poorak]-3 and Rechaka-5. Bahya Kumbhak [optional-10]

Patanjali Kriya
Hath yoga includes all of the above practices and Shuddhi Kriya.
Gyan yoga means Dhyan and Dharana.
Note – Each asana or Kriya should be performed with total focus on the sensations that arise in the body. Every movement should be easy and slow and with a flow. Every feeling should be full of happiness.

DHYAN AND DHARANA

Mindfulness Meditation is the term coined by Dr. Richard Davidson, Professor of Psychiatry, and Wisconsin University, USA. Author has termed BK-Rajayoga as Internal silence [Antar mauna] oriented mindfulness meditation.

BK- Rajayoga- Meditation

It has some similarities with Spiritually augmented Cognitive Behavioral Therapy [S.A.C.B.T.] which is the latest in Psychiatry for mind empowerment.

Brahma Kumaris Rajayoga technique as taught in 11500 BK-centres in 140 countries has the following essential components. Each component augments the beneficial effect of other components. Hence the technique is of paramount importance. *[Vidhi se hi siddhi hai]*. Miraculous benefits are obtained within three months if the technique is followed fully and totally. The schedule should form the total and **indispensible component of daily routine** of a practitioner to derive maximum benefits. This is the much needed lifestyle **modification** today.

Essential Components of BK- Lifestyle

A] **Amrit vela Meditation** at 4am to 5am regularly without break. This period of time is known in scriptures as Brahma muhurtha.

B] Traffic control- A **brief Meditation** for just one minute every one hour. This helps to restore elevated consciousness that is usually lost in the present atmosphere of gross negativity.

C] A brief meditation for ten to fifteen minutes before going to sleep. It wipes out the negative transcription of the mind and ensures a deep and refreshing sleep.

D] News Papers and TV serials give a constant and huge diet of toxic emotions. They should be avoided in the morning and two hours before going to sleep. Toxic emotions and negative thoughts deplete Prana or Life Force Energy. Both of them initiate a subtle onslaught of Free radicals or Terror molecules on Longevity genes. This results in **early ageing**, cataracts and heart attacks.

E] Satvik Paushtik vegetarian food is essential but not compulsory. Food should be prepared and eaten in a happy atmosphere and in remembrance of God. Whole focus [Mindfulness] should be on food and on the act of eating. Thus watching TV serial during eating is strictly prohibited. But for the modern man with TV-addiction this may be difficult. **Mind control by meditation shall help you.**

F] Satsang- Daily visit to a BK centre for listening to Celestial **Murali is considered as the food for the soul or Atman.**-

Murali is a Divine four page script that gives a regular input of **powerfully positive** and motivating thoughts from **Supreme Soul** [Param Atma].The **miraculous mind empowerment** by this simple ritual has to be **personally experienced to be believed. Dr. Naras Bhat ,USA**, in his excellent book entitled Stress Physiology quotes that any positive thought repeated for sizeable duration[may be half an hour or more] for **21 days** is embedded deeply in psyche and brings about a positive behavioral change. No wonder **the figure 21 chosen by Shri Ganesh is very auspicious.**

One can access the Muralis on internet or by watching 24 hours Peace of Mind channel on TV.

TRAFFIC CONTROL
A BRIEF ONE MINUTE MEDITATION EVERY ONE HOUR OR SO

Bring your consciousness to get focused in the centre of the forehead, in between the two eye brows. This is the site for **Agya Energy Chakra**. This is also the site for the Third eye or a spiritual eye. So Har har Mahadeva means each one of us has a **Third eye**. When it opens in Divine guidance during meditation, all of our negativity gets burnt out.

A single auto suggestion needs to be repeated for the whole one minute-
"I am a peaceful soul. I am a loveful soul, blissful soul, pure soul or powerful soul. I am a soul and I am not this body. I am the metaphysical conscient point of light situated at Agya chakra."

The technique involves visualizing each particular quality of the soul and **dwelling in its "Experience"** for some time. This "Experience" then gets imbibed into your psyche or subconscious mind. This implant of a seed of a thought sprouts automatically when the circumstances require that particular quality. Eg. In an encounter with a troublesome person the qualities of peace, power and compassion get emerged. Soon it has a tranquilizing effect on that troubled soul and the situation is saved. Russian R & D institutes attribute this effect to thought vibrations emanating from the soul of a Sadhak [practitioner].

Human mind is experiential. All of its permanent learning happens by acquiring "Experience." Spiritual knowledge is the conglomerate of "Collective Experiences" and "Mystical experiences [Sakshatkars]" of highly enlightened and evolved souls.

LONG VERSION- RAJAYOGA MINDFULNESS BASED STRESS REDUCTION PROGRAMME [R-M.B.S.R.P.]

MEDITATION DONE AT AMRUT VELA [4am for one hour]

PREAMBLE-
The place fixed for meditation should be the same every day. A pure and powerful atmosphere is created around that place by powerful positive thoughts emanating from Atman during meditation.

Sit comfortably with a straight back on a chair. Sukhasana or Padmasan postures on a mat are the best. This posture keeps the **seven energy** chakras of the body in same alignment. This ensures a free **flow of cosmic energy** through seven energy chakras from the top to bottom- Sahasara, Agya, Vishuddhi, Anahat, Manipura, Swadhishthan and Muladhar chakra. These energy chakras are actually the distribution points [D.P.] for **life-force energy** [Prana]. The flow of cosmic energy is called as Cosmic Vibrational Healing Whisper by Dr.

Naras Bhat, a cardiologist and a Mind Body Medicine Specialist in USA. Now perform abdominal type of breathing ten times. This process helps to calm down

R-M.B.S.R.P. involves following techniques:-
A] **Cyber scan** of own thoughts
B] **Heart felt Resonance Imaging [H.R.I.]**- shows the predominant thought or thoughts occupying one's mind and reveals the "Experience" or sensations one's Self or Atman is getting from such thoughts. Vipassana, Buddhist form of Meditation by Lord Gautama Buddha calls this process as "Differential perception." A negative thought or emotion always creates a bad feeling or sensation. Predominant thought forms a Primary Motivational Factor [P.M.F.]for the Atman. Therefore **Bhagavad Gita** tells us that a thought form the seed of our karma and destiny.
C] Auto-suggestions or self-hypnosis
D] Visualization or guided imagery.

E] STEPS OF LONG VERSION MEDITATION

1. Focus
2. Internalization
3. Cosmic Communion.
4. Post Meditation Suggestions [PMS]

First step-   Focus- Bahya Tratak-
Repeat each of the autosuggestions ten times. Visualize whatever words are spoken in the commentary.eg. I am an Ananda swaroop soul. Visualize the moment when you were full of happiness.

A] Give an auto-suggestion number one- I am a soul. **I am not this body.**
I the soul am a metaphysical conscient point of light which is immortal, indestructible and diseaseless. I a conscient of point of light am situated in the centre of the forehead in between two eye brows..
I am a peaceful, loveful, blissful, powerful and **pure** soul.

Purity has three levels-
1] Brahmacharya Celibacy- This is the purity at the level of body consciousness. It is required in **Balya Avastha** or learning phase of life. Our own research [Aurangabad] has proved that chewing five leaves of **Neem** daily helps to achieve celibacy.

Grihasthashram is governed by the rules pertaining to it.

Vanaprastha avastha means a process of withdrawing our consciousness from the external to the internal world. This is an inner **ever blissful voyage** into the fourth dimension- spiritual dimension.

Sanyas- means developing such ruling and controlling power over one's mind that the temptations, attractions and pressures of the external world fail to affect us. This is the state of spiritual equilibrium **[Sthit-pragnya avastha].** Dadi Janaki , the 100 years old Head of the Brahma kumaris has been certified by neurologists as the most stable mind in the whole world.

2] Purity at the level of thought- Ruling and controlling power over the mind is so powerful that not even one impure thought for any soul arises in the mind.

3] Highest level of purity- when you constantly have only the thoughts about the welfare of all the other persons or animals coming in contact with you. **[Shubh chintan and Shubh chintak]**

Note- A stage may come by the repeated autosuggestions when you shall lose all of the body consciousness and may "Experience" a belief that you a mere conscient point of light. However, achieving this stage requires a very long spiritual effort. But it is also true that till such a **body less state [Ashariri avastha]** is achieved by the consciousness a lifestyle following **Straight Path or Sirat al Mustaqim** takes care of your health, wealth, mental peace and happiness.

B] Now turn your attention to your thoughts.

They usually are running like superfast train in men with very high I.Q. today.
Give autosuggestion for ten times that the speed of thought is getting slower and slower.

C] Now turn your attention to your consciousness-
Perform a detail **Cyberscan** of your thoughts and categorize them into negative and waste thoughts, toxic emotions, positive thoughts and positive emotions. A rough percentage of positive and negative thoughts at this point time shall help to judge your progress and effect of spiritual effort. Perform **HRI-Heartfelt Resonance Imaging** to decide about the most predominant negative thought/emotion in your mind.
Give autosuggestion-   Let go .Don't get attached to thoughts. The speed of thoughts is gradually reducing.
Now turn your attention to your consciousness [Energy plus awareness].It is scattered like a diffuse sunlight. So it is ineffective.

Give autosuggestion-   My consciousness is getting focused on me, the conscient point of light in the centre of the forehead. Soon a single pointed focused state of consciousness shall be obtained.

As the focus increases the speed of thoughts shall get proportionately reduced. You shall be able to distinguish between the positive, negative and the waste thoughts as well as toxic emotions.[Daniel Goleman]. Desires, Toxic emotions, negative thoughts and waste thought are responsible for the depletion of your pranik strength [Life Force].

Give autosuggestion- All of my desires, toxic emotions, negative thoughts and waste thoughts are getting burnt out in the intense fire of my meditation [Yogagni].All of this negativity of mind is getting permanently deleted from my mind's computer.

A stage shall come when all the negativity shall get deleted from the mind's computer for one particular moment. When this happens, internalization of the consciousness takes place.

SECOND STEP OF R-MBSRP- Internalization

Internalization of consciousness is indicated by a feeling of totally relaxed states of mind and body with a state of bliss. Dr. Herbert Benson, an American cardiologist who founded the first Institute of Mind and Body Medicine in 1970, uses two terms for denoting these states-

1] Biological Relaxation Response **BRR** [Shavasana] and
2] The zone.**[Ekagra Chitta Avastha].**

This state of consciousness, a soul conscious or Satvik state is very important.

1] Various autosuggestions become most powerful and effective in this state.

2] Rejuvenating neuro hormones FROM THE BRAIN are secreted in this state.

3] Delta waves of deep sleep pattern are recorded usually after a regular practice [sadhana] of 2 years.

4] Lactic acid giving tiredness is quickly metabolized.

5] Secretion of stress hormones and free radicals stops.

6] Potentiation of immune system happens giving a quantum jump in resistance to infections, cancer cells, allergens and auto-antigens.

7] A quantum Jump in self-determination [Will power], Quality of Life [QOL] and E.E.H. value of life [Energy, Enthusiasm and happiness] happens.

Proof of the pudding lies in tasting it. This is known as "Experiential evidence" which has been in use for tasting the effectiveness of medicinal herbs in Ayurveda. The need for expensive state of art equipment to demonstrate an "Experience" by the practitioner of Yog- Transcendental experience." becomes redundant. One can discover whole of God instead of one God's particle if one has belief and faith.

Medical wing of Brahma kumaris [R.E.R.F.- Rajayoga Education and Research Foundation]has some novel instruments- 1] Thought graph machine [in S.P.A.R.C.

wing], 2] Aura scanner 3] Happiness index machine and 4] RespErate . However, these instruments require scientific validation by recognized research institutes.

Some Prototypes of disease-specific autosuggestions

1] Anger management- My anger and irritation has disappeared permanently from my mind's computer. I always remember that I am a peaceful, loveful and blissful soul.

2] Stress management- I am a peaceful, loveful and powerful soul. So the stress, tension, anxiety, worry fear or frustration can never contaminate my Satvik consciousness.

3] R-MBSRT for the prevention and cure of the cancer- One cancer cell is formed after each 10 raised to 17 cell divisions. Natural Killer cells [NK-cells] are the James Bond of the body. They quickly identify and destroy the cancer cell that has been formed. Hence most of us are cancer free till the last breath. So these autosuggestions may prevent cancer.

Autosuggestion and visualization for prevention and cure of cancer-

A cosmic energy, a cosmic healing Vibrational healing whisper is entering my body through the top most Sahasara energy chakra and passing through all the subsequent energy chakras – Agya, Vishuddhi, Anahat,

Manipura, Swadhishthan and Muladhar chakra and bringing a rejuvenation. The fire of meditation is so intense that this cosmic energy is burning out each and every cancer cell in my body. NK-cells in my body are quickly discovering the newly formed cancer cells and destroying them. Thus I am attaining a cancer free state.

4] For De-addiction programme-
All of the addictions happen because of stress after stress, lack of mental peace and happiness in life. So the autosuggestions focus on mental peace and happiness.
Autosuggestion -1- I am a peaceful, loveful and blissful soul. I am so powerful that I can easily resist the urge to drink or smoke for getting a temporary "High".

Autosuggestion-2- The neuro-hormones, DHEA, endorphins and Anandamide are natural and most powerful pain killers and mood elevators. So my feeling of unhappiness is disappearing from my mind. The sense of feeling good is so powerful that I shall never indulge in my addiction which gives only a temporary "High."

5] Performance enhancement-
As the Scientist Mind achieves silence [Antar-mauna] lateral thinking or Out Of Box thinking begins. This is

responsible for intuition [gut feeling or sixth sense] which enhances the power of split second best decision for the problem solving. The suggestion comes to the mind in a split second as if from cosmos. Creativity of the mind is enhanced which could be of great help in innovation. Artists may create such supreme designs or painting which may appear beyond the scope of human thinking. A man can achieve anything if he has a mind to do it.

Third step of R-MBSRP - Cosmic Communion

Visualization or guided imagery plays a great role in this step.

Visualize that I, the soul, a conscient point of light have come out of my body of five elements and undertaken a cosmic travel to Supreme abode [Param Dham] of all the souls. All of us are mere guests on this planet earth. We descend on the planet earth in the costume or body to play our respective roles in a huge world drama. The costume, the type of life and the role are decided by our past karmic accounts. Good karmic account means happiness, health and harmony. Bad karmic account means diseases, defects, early deaths, accidents, pain and suffering. A human being thus always has two choices in life. Right choice means happy and healthy life.

I am now travelling through the world of stars, moon and the sun. I have now arrived in the Micro-world of the Trinity- Brahma, the Creator and Governor, Vishnu the operator and Mahesh the Destroyer. Mahesh destroys the negativity in my mind. I now enter into Param Dham after taking the blessings from the Trinity.

In Param Dham I am experiencing a joy and peace that is beyond words. I am surrounded by a reddish yellow rejuvenating light. I am now standing in front of God, Shiva, Shiva baba, Who is Supreme Father of all the souls, Supreme teacher and Supreme Sadgatidata data.

He is also a Conscient Point of Light and incorporeal. He is a Point in appearance but an ocean of peace, happiness, power and of everything one desires in life. I am His beloved son/daughter. So whatever He has, I have a birth right over it. Red rays of power and white rays of peace and purity are emanating from the Supreme Soul [Param-Atma].I am imbibing theses rays and becoming more powerful and peaceful.

Visualize this scene for quite some time.

Visualize that I am getting richer and richer in eights powers that are necessary in life. The power of tolerance is most essential. But if while tolerating one gets a constant feeling that only "I" am tolerating and suffering then it is not true tolerance. Cosmic Universal laws tell that acquiring one power attracts other powers as if from Cosmos. Power of judgment and right decision is another very important power of the soul. An "Inner voice" always shouts loudly when a man is about to commit wrong. The right or wrong is decided by eternal cosmic laws. Enhanced power of judgment is necessary for the best solutions to the problems in life. Power of accommodation, co-operation, condensation and power to face and finish are other important powers one acquires in cosmic communion with Supreme Father.

Now I after getting enriched with power and peace I am undertaking the return journey. I have crossed the

Micro-world of Trinity and also the world of Sun, Moon and stars. Now I have come to rest on my eternal seat in between the two eye brows.

Visualize- The rays and vibrations of power, peace, purity, love and bliss are spreading through each and every cell of the body rejuvenating and re-charging them. Dwell in this "Experience" for some time.

Post Meditation Suggestions

Now give two auto suggestions to the mind-

1] Let me remain in this elevated powerful soul conscious state throughout the day while performing my tasks under any circumstances which may try to disturb this state of consciousness.

2] Next day, at 4am, Amrit –vela when I begin my meditation [yog with Supreme Soul] let me begin from this elevated state of consciousness so that with each day I shall become more powerful, peaceful, loveful, blissful and pure.

APPENDIX – II

Pranayam Motivated Defaecation

A recent survey has shown that 14% of all Indians including the young suffer from mild to severe constipation. Severe constipation is very common in senior age group or the patients in Geriatric O.P.D. Several have to take enema on regular basis. Some have an experience of taking out the faecal nuggets with fingers. Lack of exercise, Pizza Burger Cola diet and Non-vegetarian diet are some of the important contributing factors. Over use of Over The Counter [OTC] pills or purgatives weaken the walls of intestine. Shortly it results in weak peristalsis or propelling movement of the intestine.

Hydrotherapy prior to P.M.D. Programme-
Warning- Never strain while defecating if you wish to avoid piles or fissures. Everything in yogic practices is done with ease.

Prior hydrotherapy- It is necessary to hydrate oneself well one day prior to P.M.D. Drink a minimum of 15 to 20 glasses of water throughout the day. It is necessary to drink water even if one is not thirsty. This is because with advancing age, the reflex initiating the drinking process gets progressively weaker. **The test for**

adequate hydration is that the urine always remains clear like water. Henceforth make it a practice to drink plenty of water throughout your life.

Jal Dhauti is a yogic kriya if performed for one month ensures adequate hydration and effective purging out of accumulated toxins.

Take four to five glasses of water or more if you can, no sooner one gets up at 4am.[Amrit-vela]. Warm water with a pinch of salt is helpful initially. A session of Pranayam after Amrit-vela meditation should be followed by P.M.D. Isabgol at night may help but required only initially. Learning Shuddhi kriyas like Jal Dhauti and Pranayam called Agnisaar helps.

Relaxation of mind by meditation plays a significant role. Never sing – Tu atki hai kanha, main tadapata yanha. This creates a negative programming of your mind. Instead sing. ,"Chal akela chal akela, Tera maila peeche chchuta, tu chal akela. This shall be a positive programming of your mind for the task at hand.

Do not contaminate the elevated Satvik consciousness achieved by meditation by taking a newspaper or your problems to the toilet seat. Focus your attention on your colon. Here the single pointed focus achieved by meditation helps greatly. Visualize about a faecal bolus stuck up at the appendix side of the colon. Now breathing deeply [abdominal breathing] visualize that the bolus is gradually getting unstuck. Now it is moving forward with each progressive contraction of the colon. Agnisaar at this point of time helps. Visualize that the bolus is now travelling in the ascending colon. Now it has entered the Transverse colon. Its forward movement has now become quicker. Visualize that now the bolus has entered descending colon and speedily going to the end of the rectum. Now a final push and it is out of the body. Do not strain at this point of time as it may cause piles to form. Each process has to be done with ease without straining at any point. Immense relief and joy at this point of time is beyond words. In fact you shall also see the relief writ large on the faces of the people around you, especially in an elevator.

Within a month you shall be colon trained and defecation shall be as easy as taking a breath.

BK- Rajayoga restores the SNS Versus PNS balance [Sympathetic Nervous System and Parasympathetic Nervous System] which is usually disturbed in Diabetes. This is the common cause of constipation in Diabetics.

Disturbed Internal balance of ions, sugar and lipids also contribute to N.C.D.s like Head ache, Migraine, Acidity, High B.P., Diabetes and Heart attacks.

Gut Like Protein –I and II released from Gastro intestinal tract helps in controlling appetite in Diabetes.

Medical science behind each and every ancient yogic practice needs to be investigated by a systematic research in Medical Institutes. There is a paucity of this type of research because the Indians themselves have stopped believing in the ancient Indian spiritual wisdom. Whole of the world is engaged in yog while Indians are pursuing the lifestyle of Bhog and Rog.

18-02-2019

                                    BK Dr. Dilip V. Kaundinya

www.ingramcontent.com/pod-product-compliance
Lightning Source LLC
Chambersburg PA
CBHW031308060426
42444CB00032B/417